Keith Hill is a New Zealand writer and channeller whose work explores the intersection of mysticism, history, science, religion and psychology. His books include *The God Revolution*, *Striving To Be Human*, and *Practical Spirituality*, each of which won the Ashton Wylie Award, New Zealand's premiere prize for spiritual writing. Since 2008 he has been working with fellow channeller Peter Calvert to present a range of teachings and practices offered by two non-embodied spiritual entities. Keith's most recent book is *The New Mysticism*.

Reviews of *The God Revolution*

"Hill's exposition is a fine example of scrupulously rigorous scholarship – it is remarkable how much ground is covered within his brief historical survey. ... An impressive and accessible introduction to a challenging philosophical topic. " – Kirkus Review

"Keith Hill is a writer in the vein of Karen Armstrong ... The prize that celebrates New Zealand's forward thinkers is thoroughly deserved." – Mike Alexander, Sunday Star Times

"A scholarly yet accessible book. ... Deserves to be read by all those who care about ideas, the trajectory of civilization and its future form." – Peter Dornauf, www.eyecontact.com

BOOKS BY KEITH HILL

NON-FICTION
The New Mysticism
The God Revolution
Striving To Be Human

FICTION
The Ecstasy of Cabeza de Vaca
Puck of the Starways
Blue Kisses

MYSTICAL POETRY
The Bhagavad Gita: A New Poetic Version
Walking Without Feet:
Selected Poetry of Mirabai and Kabir
Psalms of Exile and Return

CHANNELLED
What Is Really Going On?
Where Do I Go When I Meditate?
Experimental Spirituality
Practical Spirituality
Psychological Spirituality

WITH PETER CALVERT
The Matapaua Conversations
The Kosmic Web

PRACTICAL SPIRITUALITY

Keith Hill

attar books

First published by Attar Books 2018
Copyright © Keith Hill 2018
The moral rights of the author have been asserted.

Paperback ISBN 978-0-9951059-0-4
Hardcover ISBN 978-0-9951059-2-8
Ebook ISBN 978-0-9951059-1-1

Cover designed by Abigail Kerr

All rights reserved. Copying and distributing passages excerpted from this book for the purpose of sharing and debating is permitted on the condition that (1) the source of each excerpt is fully acknowledged and (2) the excerpts are given not sold, ie. the process is non-commercial. Otherwise, except for fair dealing or brief passages quoted in a newspaper, magazine, radio, television or internet review, no part of this book may be reproduced in any form or by any means without permission in writing from the Publisher.

Attar Books
www.attarbooks.com   www.experimentalspirituality.net

CONTENTS

FROM THE GUIDES   7

PART ONE: SPIRIT AND ITS EXPRESSION

1. On Becoming Spiritual — 13
2. The Seven Core Dispositions — 21
3. Modality and Secondary Disposition — 33
4. The Model of the Five-Layered Self — 39
5. The Essence Self — 48
6. The Socialised Self — 56
7. The Momentum of Everyday Identity — 67

PART TWO: REINCARNATION AND THIS LIFE

8. What Is the Purpose of a Life? — 83
9. Reincarnation and Deep Essence — 88
10. The Impact of Karma — 94
11. The Seven Life Goals — 106
12. The Life Plan and Life Lessons — 122
13. The Trade-offs of Being Embodied — 128
14. Incarnation and Growing to Maturity — 134

PART THREE: MASTERING THE ART OF INCARNATION

15. How a Life Plan Manifests — 147
16. Confronting Negativities — 153
17. Nurturing the Positives — 160
18. Addressing the Reality of Your Life — 166

GLOSSARY   175

From the Guides

THIS IS THE SECOND IN A SERIES of five books that explore the process of becoming spiritual outside a religious context. The first book, *Experimental Spirituality*, proposed that your incarnation on Earth and subsequent journey through life may be viewed as an experiment. Not an experiment anyone else is performing on you but an experiment you yourself are carrying out, over an extended sequence of lives, as you explore the numerous possible activities, roles and relationships that may be experienced in the human realm.

As a consequence, the process of entering a body is not haphazard. Before incarnation each spirit decides on a principal goal or set of goals, selects psychological traits that will facilitate achieving the goal or goals, and generates a life plan that may, or may not, be followed during the course of living the chosen life. There are reasons for both outcomes. This book examines why this is so, along with the pre-birth planning process and how planning impacts on your current life.

Because of the numerous factors involved in all this, and because the human psychospiritual make-up is complex, the most significant psychological aspects that affect human incarnation will be examined over two books. In this book we introduce a number of key psychological factors in relation to the life plan. In the next book, *Psychological Spirituality*, other central factors will be examined in the context of true and false personalities.

Achieving understanding of how your psychology functions is essential because self-defensive behaviours ensure that the majority of human beings remain locked into shallow, limited and entirely reactive perceptions of their life situation. As a result they are unable to see what drives their selected experiences. We use the phrase "selected experiences" deliberately, because all human beings select the major elements of their life experiences, whether prior to incarnating or during the course of their life.

As was the case with *Experimental Spirituality*, this is a channelled book. The "we" referred to in the previous paragraph is a non-embodied spiritual entity that has lived out its cycle of incarnations on this planet and now offers observations derived from having personally experienced the human domain in all its fullness and variety. Our purpose is to help those who are curious about their existence to better understand what is occurring to them during the course of their life.

There are many very different ways to consider human existence. Historically, much has been made of human life on Earth as ultimately being a mystery. This mystery manifests in the feelings people have that their existence is not as it seems, the realisation that sense experience is not the only kind of experience, and from the appreciation that human existence is more layered than everyday perception allows. In practice, mysterious feelings constitute anomalous experiential data that most people tend to explain, or rather explain away, using received wisdom, whether that received wisdom be religious, materialist, scientific, rationalist, New Age, or atheist in nature. Usually such explanations are no more than stabs in the dark, but people cling to them as a means of calming themselves so they may avoid having to dig more deeply into their otherwise somewhat disturbing experiences and questions. By this process easy answers are used to cover uneasy doubts. Yet the mystery of being human remains.

In this series of books we seek to demystify the spiritual aspects of human existence. In doing so we have deliberately avoided using traditional religious and spiritual concepts and language. This is not because religions and spiritual traditions are wrong. It is merely because all established traditions present a mixture of valid and invalid concepts and explanations. Rather than attempt the huge task of sifting what is useful to today's spiritual enquirers from what is not, in this series we have chosen to avoid traditional language altogether and instead present material designed to make sense to twenty-first century spiritual enquirers using largely familiar terms. Hence, in a very open sense, and certainly without claiming that this is in any way definitive, we offer a new approach to age-old human experiences, questions and dilemmas.

Yet in saying this what is offered is not entirely new. And here we need to introduce our scribe, Keith Hill. Over the course of this individual's current life he has accumulated, through his own efforts, an extensive understanding of a range of psychospiritual concepts and practices. This is due to his exposure to the Gurdjieff Work along with Sufi meditation practices. He also spent time in Rajasthan studying Indian spirituality. And over the years he has pursued his own lines of enquiry.

In addition, we have guided him towards certain materials that we consider useful to today's spiritual enquirers. These materials have aided our scribe in his personal quest to develop a contemporary framework for understanding human psychospiritual nature. His increased understanding has in turn assisted us in our self-selected task of attempting to clarify the nature of human life and spirituality. The *Bhagavad Gita* is one set of additional material towards which we guided our scribe. Another is the collection of channelled writings that have become known as the Michael Teachings. This body of literature was designed, in part, to extend the Gurdjieff Work to accommodate the process of reincarnation. Given our scribe's prior experiences, he found this material particularly attractive.

In drawing on these materials, and others that perceptive readers will undoubtedly recognise, the point needs to be made that no one owns any of these ideas or teachings. Genuine information emanates from the spiritual domain into the human physical and social realms. Enquiring individuals may find information emanating from the spiritual domain in books or by talking to others who have discovered it for themselves. At times information arrives into individuals' awareness from their own spiritual self, whether during meditation, in quiet moments, when thinking or feeling intensely about an issue, or via dreams. And sometimes the energetic self is a vehicle for information that arrives from beyond the individual, as here.

When received information has a significant impact on individuals they naturally become attached to the medium via which it was received. Hence people become attached to certain books, to individual teachers, to groups, to processes, or to particular teachings. Intense attachment leads to a sense of ownership. But, of course, no one can or does own anything of a spiritual nature. Indeed, genuine spiritual sharing involves freely giving what one has to others who need it. And we are referring here to freely giving in a psychological sense much more than in a material sense.

If you are drawn to the range of ideas that are presented throughout this series, as well as in other books that we have already and will in the future cause to be written, and if you recognise materials that are presented in either familiar or unfamiliar ways, we ask you to approach these ideas afresh. Certainly draw on what you know to evaluate what you read. But also use this material to re-examine what you know. Use it to help you uncover new information in the experiential stock you have already built up during the duration of your life to date – or, we should more exactly say, your *lives* to date.

As part of our task of helping enquiring individuals achieve a clear understanding of who, what, where and why they are, in *Experimental Spirituality* we challenged readers to collect observational data on themselves in relation to their fears and what gives them bliss.* Before continuing reading this book we suggest you carry out this exercise. Why? Because it relates directly to the material presented in Chapters One and Two, and it will help you use what is stated there to understand your own spiritual nature.

As is observed in the following pages, *being* spiritual is straight forward, because you already are a spirit. However, *becoming* spiritual, that is, becoming consciously aware of your own spiritual core and how it manifests in your life, including how it has planned the experiment that is your current incarnation, is another matter. We send this, the second book of our series on spirituality, into the human domain with the hope that it will help all to better understand the circumstances of their existence, and that you, the seeker of understanding, may more effectively explore and develop all that you are.

---

* The challenge was included in Chapter Thirteen of *Experimental Spirituality*. It is also available on the website: www.experimentalspirituality.net.

PART ONE

SPIRIT AND ITS EXPRESSION

CHAPTER 1

On Becoming Spiritual

THIS CHAPTER BEGINS WITH A WARNING. Becoming spiritual is not easy. Learning what your personal life plan is, understanding what you are here to achieve during the course of this particular lifetime, and deciding how to live in order to best give expression to your deepest spiritual aims, is no easily accomplished task.

There are many barriers to understanding who you are and how you function as an individual. There are further barriers to putting hard won understanding into action in daily living. Some of these barriers are external, consisting of socially and religiously constructed taboos regarding what you may legitimately delve into. One is projected fear, which is a control mechanism that stops you entering deeply into yourself. If you are reading this we can assume you have already overcome the majority of these external barriers.

However, the most significant barriers, and the most difficult to overcome, are internal. They consist of the various defensive behaviours of denying, justifying, deflecting and attacking that exist within your own psychological make-up. In order to become aware of your life plan you first need to identify your inner nature. And to identify your inner nature you need to confront and overcome these inner barriers.

Because the way these inner barriers function is multi-levelled and devious, analysis of them needs to be detailed. So while this book has been written as clearly as possible, the detail it contains regarding the mechanisations of the human psychospiritual make-up itself presents yet another barrier.

That is why this chapter begins with a warning. In places what follows is complex and dense. But it needs to be in order to do justice to the complexity of human awareness and in order to offer a practical way of delving into and changing that complexity.

So, if you have taken this warning on board, and you are willing to appreciate that this book will only make sense to you to the degree that you are willing to spend time comprehending what it elucidates of your inner make-up, and you further appreciate that the cycle of understanding will only be completed when you apply what is presented here to your own life, then we may happily proceed.

YOU ARE A SPIRITUAL BEING

Whether you wish to be one or not, you are a spiritual being. Whether you acknowledge it or not, you have a spiritual dimension at the core of your identity. This means that being spiritual is not a big deal. You don't require a special initiation from those in the know. You already are a spirit every moment of your existence. Furthermore, this reality is not reliant on you knowing it. Whatever your beliefs, whatever your outlook on life, whether you deny or affirm it, you possess a spirit that, at all times and in all situations, functions deep within you according to its particular nature.

Of course, not everyone is aware of their spiritual dimension. For some spirit is a fact of daily existence experienced when meditating or praying, or when sharing with others, when looking at the stars in the night sky, or when listening to a moving piece of music. For others spirit is felt only during moments of extreme emotion or physical duress. Yet others have no conscious experience of spirit at all. Naturally, not experiencing spirit doesn't mean it isn't there.

This means there is a difference between being a spirit and being spiritual. *Being a spirit* is a fact of human existence that is the case whether it is known or not. *Becoming spiritual* requires an intent to consciously engage with spirit and make a sustained effort to connect your everyday self with your spiritual self.

The task of becoming spiritual is achieved in a variety of ways. Historically, human beings have used meditation, worship and prayer, bodily austerities, yoga, martial arts, daily work, psychotherapies and intellectual study to enhance their spiritual understanding. This book outlines a psycho-spiritual approach to becoming spiritual that uses the human psychological make-up as a springboard into experiencing spirit. It involves coming to an appreciation of why you are the way you are, why you behave as you do, and why your life follows the paths it does. A key factor is understanding your life goal and life plan and appreciating how they impact on the choices you make.

Because each human being is already a spirit, this approach to becoming spiritual begins wherever you are living right now. And it proceeds in whichever direction you are already travelling. So you don't have to go anywhere in particular, or live in any special way, or give assent to any particular words, in order to practise it. This approach doesn't require you to change your lifestyle. You can keep doing what you already do. But you do need to transform your perception, understanding and intention while doing so. Books such as this can be used to stimulate, and even facilitate, inner transformation. So can identifying those concepts and motives that underpin your everyday self and expand or close down your perception and understanding. Discernment is always required of those who would become spiritual.

What all this adds up to is that at your core you are a spiritual identity. Of course, you consciously and knowingly experience this only occasionally, if at all, but because you are a spiritual identity spirit is always present in your daily living. Becoming spiritual, which in this case means using a psychospiritual process to delve into what is occurring within you, will enable you to appreciate and understand your core spiritual nature. This is done by building a bridge between the everyday self and the spiritual self, with the spiritual self eventually actively participating in your everyday life.

In short, becoming spiritual is the task of becoming a more competent and knowing owner-operator of a body and of its core spiritual identity.

YOUR LIFE JOURNEY AS A BUS RIDE

What prevents you from gaining knowledge of, and so directly experiencing, your core spiritual identity? What is the primary barrier to transforming your perception, understanding and intention? You are. You are the barrier that prevents you from realising who, what and why you are.

In order to appreciate how the barrier operates, envisage your life journey as a bus ride. Bus travel is straight forward. You go to a bus stop and wait for a bus. When one drives up, you climb on board, pay the fare, ride for a distance, and alight when it reaches where you wish to go. However, for that journey to be possible a complex series of activities has already occurred.

First, the bus needs to exist. This means that the design, engineering and building of the bus coach has taken place. Additionally, a public or private transportation company, having worked through all the regulations, laws, fees and employment issues, has: purchased the bus and has a business plan to pay operating costs; designed and published schedules and timetables; and organised ticket signage, advertising and purchasing. So while catching a bus is a very simple activity, the organisation behind getting a bus to a specific stop at a certain time, and so delivering passengers to their destinations, involves a complex interplay of intensely organised activities.

This scenario equally applies to your life journey. Long before you were born the human species had evolved on this planet. Then, over the millennia, as human numbers increased, and as individuals worked together in increasingly sophisticated ways, humanity's ancient forebears organised orderly food production, built towns and cities, laid roads, and established communities of all kinds. Each individual is born into particular languages, laws, systems of education, religions and social practices. So each life journey occurs within a complex web of pre-existing conditions.

You need a map, a schedule and money in order to make the most of bus travel. Similarly, to make the most of the opportunity of being a spiritual identity "riding" a body, you need the psychospiritual equivalents of maps, schedules and money. These are perception, knowledge and intention. With these you can journey, experience places, and live a satisfying life. Without them a life journey remains timid, uncertain, and ultimately unsatisfying.

The question then arises: Why bother to consider these deeper aspects of human existence? Since everyone already possesses a spirit, what's the point in developing deeper spiritual perception, knowledge and intention? What's the purpose of becoming spiritual? If everyone is already on a life journey, why spend time and effort trying to comprehend how the bus was built, what routes are available, and what the full array of destinations are? Why can't individuals just keep to their current habitual life schedule, go where their body and life circumstances take them, and leave it at that?

This is where the earlier statement that you are the barrier becomes relevant. Because to answer a question with another question, what part of an individual is asking what is the point in making an effort? The answer is that this is a question asked by the everyday identity.

The everyday identity is immersed in everyday life. The intricacies of everyday living are all it can see. In contrast, the spiritual identity sees much deeper. But everyday identity is so caught up in its life circumstances and so involved in its reactions to those circumstances that it remains unaware of the spiritual identity's presence, let alone its aims. So it questions the validity of the deeper issues that engage the spiritual identity. In effect, there is a barrier within the human psychospiritual makeup. It is a barrier that isolates the everyday identity from the spiritual identity.

Actually, such a barrier is necessary because it enables individuals to become fully immersed in the circumstances of their life journey and so to live out the consequences of their chosen life plan. But at the same time it prevents individuals from becoming aware of their spiritual identity. It keeps them in ignorance of what they were born into a body to achieve. We call this barrier the momentum of everyday awareness.

THE BARRIER OF THE EVERYDAY

Everyday awareness is generated by the everyday identity immersed in the circumstances of everyday living. It limits the acquisition of spiritual-level experience and knowledge because it keeps human beings locked into a repetition of the familiar, the known, the comfortable, the safe. It doesn't make any difference if an individual's repetitive everyday identity is negative or positive, destructive or affirming, tough and arduous, or easy-going and soft. This is because human beings get comfortable as much with the harsh, the tough and the unrelenting as they do with their opposites. It is the repetition itself that forms the barrier. Whatever everyday experiences consist of, they generate a momentum that everyday awareness settles into. Once that happens life becomes familiar and comfortable. As a consequence, individuals remain blind to the deeper reality that underpins their existence.

Becoming spiritual is a process that changes all this. It transforms the everyday awareness of the everyday identity by filling it with the spiritual awareness of the spiritual identity. As a result, everyday life becomes imbued with spiritual presence. This is a transformation that occurs by increments, over a period of years, as spiritual awareness gradually seeps into an individual's everyday awareness. The end result is a life that is transformed from the inside out. The essential prerequisite to achieving inner transformation is intention. Without the intention to be curious, to explore, to move out of where and what you are, each of you remains stuck, limited and unknowing.

It needs to be made clear that five key assumptions underpin the psycho-spiritual approach to transforming and spiritualising everyday perceptions and understanding. These assumptions need to be identified before we start.

FIVE KEY ASSUMPTIONS

First, as we have already asserted, at their core each human being is a spiritual identity. Each individual spiritual identity exists within, but is not identical to, a physical body. This implies that a human being, as spiritual identity, existed before its body was born and will continue to exist after it dies.

Second, because human beings are fundamentally spiritual identities, they do not live just one life in one body. Human spiritual identities live many lives in many bodies. Reincarnation is assumed here as a fact of spiritual being.

Third, the purpose of reincarnation is for individuals to gain experience, to expand understanding, and, to put it simply, to get better at what they do. Just as anyone becomes better at any task through practice, so all become better at being an embodied spiritual identity through repeatedly trying their hand at the numerous and varied possibilities that being human facilitates. By practising, each spiritual identity acquires skills, knowledge and understanding and learns to better love and share. Because these behaviours and traits are difficult to achieve, and because the human domain is a complex and difficult place for spiritual identities to navigate through, no one gets everything right at the first try. Repeated incarnations are required. As with everything else in the human domain, only practice makes perfect.

Fourth, with each incarnation every embodied spirit has a psychologically oriented life goal and a simple or intricate life plan. But the problem is:

Fifth, when spiritual identities enter a body they forget what and who they are and why they have incarnated in a body. As a result, they are diverted from fulfilling their goal and plan.

So a significant step in the task of becoming spiritual involves each individual remembering who they are and what they are here to achieve. This is the crux of becoming spiritual. It is easy to jump on a bus, buy a ticket and go wherever the bus takes you. It is much more difficult to move into the driver's seat and start steering the bus yourself. To drive the bus you need knowledge and skill. And you need the intent to drive the bus in the first place. Which means you need to become aware that it is possible to drive the bus, that you have that choice.

There are many barriers preventing individuals from taking charge of their life journey and implementing all aspects of their life plan. There is the momentum of everyday awareness, which needs to be changed. There are negative psychological behaviours and traits that limit everyday awareness and keep it trundling day after day down the same narrow inner streets. And there is the weight of everyday life itself, which presses down on human awareness, captures its attention, and keeps individuals asleep to, and ignorant of, their own deeper reality and possibilities.

The key is transformation. However, transformation requires not just the intent to transform, but knowledge of how to do so, along with consistent and sustained application. Together, intent, knowledge and application help human beings make the most of their life possibilities.

LIFE IS A JOURNEY

This is a book about journeying. It is about discovering new things about your self. It is about going where you haven't been before. And it is about perceiving what you haven't seen before.

At times what you find within yourself will certainly be frightening. At other times what you find will be affirming, invigorating, even ecstasy-inducing. The self contains numerous highways and by-ways. There are main streets, lanes less travelled, and cul-de-sacs. To travel through these inner streets you need to understand your self. To achieve that you need a map that indicates possible destinations and provides directions for getting there.

All this is practical. This book has been written to offer a practical means for discovering who and why you are, what you are here to achieve in this incarnation, and how to transform your life in order to achieve it. The journey begins with a consideration of the nature of spiritual identity.

CHAPTER 2

The Seven Core Dispositions

THE ONE FUNDAMENTAL ASPECT of spiritual identity of which human beings commonly remain unaware is the natural disposition of their core consciousness. Religious and spiritual traditions teach that the human spirit should serve God and be good. For religions, being good consists of obeying religious strictures, while for spiritual traditions being good involves cultivating inner virtues in order to achieve wisdom. In both cases, whether goodness or wisdom is sought, the teaching is that closeness to God then follows. And this closeness gives rise to bliss.

In all this the actual nature of the individual spirit is not explored. The traditional view is that spiritually each person is good and wise and so deserves the bliss of being close to God, or is bad and ignorant and deserves the non-bliss that results from being far from God. Putting aside the judgment that lies behind these dichotomies, this is as far as traditional religious and spiritual teachings go in describing the nature of the individual spirit. Yet these twinned criteria – good/bad, ignorant/wise – do not reflect the complexity of what occurs to human beings during the course of their lives. The fact is that many things happen that cannot automatically be put into the baskets of wise and good or bad and ignorant.

For example, everyone is naturally drawn towards certain people. But they don't know why. They just get on with them. Other people, equally inexplicably, they don't like. These grate, so are avoided. Or, if they are forced together, their presence stimulates negative emotional reactions such as anger or resentment, or feeling inferior or superior.

Everyone can look back at key moments in their lives and wonder just what they were thinking when they fell in love with that person, or went into business with another, or decided to pursue a particular course of study, or choose a career, hobby or lifestyle that permanently changed the direction of their life. Of course, sometimes circumstances turn out better than expected and people call themselves lucky, or circumstances turn out worse and they decide they're unlucky. But the reason they made those choices in the first place continues to elude them.

Equally, individuals are naturally drawn towards certain outlooks, and without thinking too much about it join groups of other people who they feel share their outlook. Whether the group is religious, ecological, political, occupational, social, musical, artistic or sports-driven, the reality is that certain ways of looking at the world seem natural to you. Yet you don't know why. And you have no idea why other people have such different outlooks to you and why they are as convinced as you are that their view is correct.

You may draw on religious, scientific, New Age or rationalist explanations as to why you respond the ways you do and make the choices you have. But the truth is they are at best guesses and at worst attempts to paper over what you do not understand by pretending that you do. The mystery that resides at the core of human experience is more subtle than what is encompassed by standard religious, scientific, New Age and rationalist explanations. Being human just is not that simple.

A key factor in all this is with respect to the different ways individuals achieve their bliss. As noted, traditional religions and spiritual traditions maintain bliss is achieved by being good and wise in obeying God. But the ways people pursue and achieve bliss are certainly not as straight forward as this suggests. In some things people are wise, in others they are ignorant. There are times when everyone does good and others when they fall well short and disappoint themselves. And, significantly, those who consider God is unimportant or even non-existent may nonetheless live highly satisfactory lives that contribute to others' well-being and growth.

To understand how each person is so different in the ways they perceive, process experiences, make decisions and seek bliss, we'll begin with a proposal regarding human spiritual nature.

Traditionally, everyone is told that all spirits are made of the same spiritual stuff, but that some spirits naturally lean towards being wise and good while others are naturally bad and ignorant. So spirits are considered to be identical in substance but to differ in their innate dispositions. What is proposed here is that human beings certainly possess an individual spiritual disposition. But this disposition is more subtle, and contains far greater variation, than is captured by the traditional terms of wise and good, bad and ignorant. In order to explore these differences, it is proposed that human beings possess one of seven core dispositions. These dispositions underpin the wide variety of ways that human beings act in the world and the very different ways that individuals seek their bliss.

WHY BLISS?

Before we go any further, why is bliss being privileged over the traditional concepts of goodness and wisdom? What is wrong with them as life goals? The answer is experience.

Living is about experiencing. During the course of a life journey, whatever is pursued, found, achieved, not achieved, gloried in, regretted, loved, or felt sadness over or compassion for, it is all grounded in personal experience. Individuals may restrict themselves to a narrow band of experiences or they may embrace a diverse range. Some people are naturally timid, others are reckless. Some enjoy the intoxication and danger of diving deep, others prefer the safety of the shore. But living is all about experience in all its vast variety. Heightened positive experiencing naturally has a qualitative value. That value is identified here as bliss. The striving to experience bliss underpins more of life experiences and life goals than people realise.

Bliss in the form of immediate sensory-based experience is called pleasure. Pleasure includes eating a tasty meal, drinking a fine wine, watching an exciting sports game, enjoying working in the garden, or completing an enjoyable task. Longer term bliss is called happiness. Happiness may result from raising a family, having a fulfilling career, watching the development and success of a family member or protégé, carrying out a long-term project, or sustaining a long-term relationship. In this sense, pleasure is experienced at the level of the biological self, while happiness is experienced by the essence self. Bliss functions at a deeper level than either pleasure or happiness. Bliss is spiritual in nature. It arises from the full expression of the deepest self. Insofar as the spirit seeks to express itself to its satisfaction during the course of its life, it is seeking bliss. And when an individual spirit achieves bliss, that experience goes right down to his or her spiritual core.

However, not all forms of bliss are the same. This is where we come to the seven fundamental core dispositions of spirit. These dispositions give rise to seven fundamentally different forms of bliss.

THE SEVEN CORE SPIRITUAL DISPOSITIONS

The following descriptions, drawn from the Michael Teachings, are attempts to capture in words realities that are elusive. They are approximations rather than full and final truths. So think of these descriptions of dispositions as metaphors that approximate the differences between individuals. With this in mind, the seven core dispositions may be thought of metaphorically as the medieval roles of servant, artisan, warrior, scholar, sage, priest and king.

THE SEVEN CORE DISPOSITIONS

	(+)	(−)
SERVANT	Service	Bondage
ARTISAN	Creation	Artifice
WARRIOR	Persuasion	Coercion
SCHOLAR	Knowledge	Theory
SAGE	Expression	Rhetoric
PRIEST	Compassion	Zeal
KING	Mastery	Tyranny

FIGURE 2.1

THE SEVEN CORE DISPOSITIONS

When you consider these dispositions be aware that they are not descriptions of social roles. Rather, these medieval metaphors attempt to capture the flavour of the seven core dispositions that influence the ways that human beings go about expressing themselves during the course of their life – and finding their bliss.

SERVANT

Those possessing the core disposition of a servant achieve their bliss by serving the common good, however the common good may be conceived. Their common good may be limited to family or embrace tribe, nation or planet. It may involve working at the level of the United Nations or be focused on fulfilling a small task in an unnoticed corner of the world.

It is possible to transform any task into an act of service. So a musician, an architect, a politician, a drain layer, a doctor, a teacher, a gardener, or the CEO of a major corporation may all manifest the servant disposition. They achieve their bliss when they inwardly transform their work into service.

A key aspect of the way servants express their core disposition is that it is through people or other creatures, such as plants or animals. So while servants have a concept or ideal of what the good is for them, they express it through their interactions with others. As a general statement (recognising all general statements have exceptions), those with the servant disposition are people's people. That is, they express themselves best in social environments, whether that involves just two or three people, an extended family, or large groups.

Those possessing the servant disposition naturally nurture others, promote fairness and justice, and bring a genuine loving warmth to the often fraught ways that human beings live, love, fight and work together. The servant finds bliss when striving to make the world a better place in which others may live.

There is a negative expression of the servant disposition. This occurs when an individual chooses a good to serve that exploits, oppresses or injures others and defends those performing such activities, or when the servant becomes too passive and ends up either being enslaved or abetting his or her abasement. We will examine how this occurs in *Psychological Spirituality*.

Famed examples of servants: Queen Victoria, Queen Elizabeth 2, Dalai Lama, Nelson Mandela, Mother Teresa.

ARTISAN

Those with an artisan disposition find their bliss in being creative. Their creativity is focused on manipulating physical materials, whether the materials consist of objects, paint, sounds, words, or even their own body. The artisan is naturally drawn towards the arts and crafts, mechanics and engineering of all sorts, athletics and sports that engineer physical performance, and sciences that focus on the natural world, such as entomology and genetics – although it must be kept in mind that a servant may just as naturally have a career as an etymologist or geneticist.

This brings us to a crucial point regarding differences in approach to the same job that differentiate the seven dispositions. A servant scientist and an artisan scientist may be engaged in exactly the same kind of biological experimentation. But where the servant is motivated by a desire to serve the common good, the artisan seeks to discover the underlying principles that unite various phenomena. The servant sensibility has a deeply embedded ethical drive, whereas the artisan sensibility seeks to find underlying patterns and structures.

An example of artisan bliss is the bliss an athlete finds in tuning his or her body to achieve the perfect performance. (Note this bliss differs from the joy of winning.) Other varieties include the bliss of an architect who works to achieve a perfect balance between form, materials, and landscape, Michelangelo's bliss as he sought to reveal the form hidden in a block of marble, and the bliss of scientists like Newton and Einstein who strove to uncover natural laws. The techno-nerd cracking computer code is engaged in artisan bliss, as is the pianist working through technical details to create a spell-binding performance.

The greatest artworks of prehistory, including Paleolithic cave paintings of animals and the stone structures and pyramids that dot the planet, were created by artisans. Artisans have shaped modern life through the mechanical gadgets they have invented. Engineering structures such as dams and bridges, and all the high-tech innovations that fill workplaces and homes, have predominantly been designed by artisans.

Examples of artisans: Michelangelo, Isaac Newton, Vincent van Gogh, Thomas Edison, Virginia Woolf, Nikola Tesla, Walt Disney, Albert Einstein, Princess Diana, Hilary Clinton, Björk.

WARRIOR

The warrior disposition finds bliss in challenges and in being at the sharp end of any activity. The Spartans are an example of the warrior disposition in action. Tough and disciplined, they were not just capable of coping with physical hardships, they enthusiastically embraced them.

A modern CEO with a warrior disposition would find bliss in the battle to take over another company or in defending his own company from a takeover bid. He or she would revel in the hurly-burly of the corporate world because of a natural inclination to confront, to strategise, and a powerful desire to prove him or herself in business combat.

Because of this, a CEO with a warrior disposition may not perform well in situations where company consolidation is required. In contrast, a CEO with a servant disposition would naturally seek to find common ground that suited all. An individual with an artisan disposition would be unlikely to seek bliss as a CEO at all, because artisans tend not to find satisfaction in managing a business. However, if the position offered an opportunity to reorganise the business structure and to coordinate all departments, that is a different matter. Henry Ford building the most efficient assembly line of its time is an example of the artisan approach to business.

Warriors love challenges. But they are also loyal. Warriors naturally fit into team environments. Team sports appeal to warriors because they offer physical and tactical challenges and require loyalty to the team ethos. Loner warriors express their loyalty by attaching themselves to a tradition, philosophy, discipline or practice, using the struggle of working outside the mainstream as a key part of their challenge.

What warriors have historically brought to human culture is the drive to set challenges and goals, then realise them. In addition, warriors tend to be grounded in the physical reality of living. So when others get too dreamy or abstract, warriors bring them back to Earth, focus their energy, and strive to facilitate practical outcomes.

The positive manifestation of the warrior disposition is their ability to be persuasive and sweep others up in their energy, enthusiasm and pragmatism. The negative manifestation of the warrior disposition is coercion, when they force others to adhere to their outlook, doctrine or discipline. Warriors' disregard for their own physical comfort can also lead them to mistreat others.

Examples of warriors: Julius Caesar, Ivan the Terrible, Richard the Third, Igor Stravinsky, Adolph Hitler, Jack London, G.I. Gurdjieff, Jane Fonda, Sigourney Weaver.

SCHOLAR

Those possessing a scholar disposition seek their bliss in acquiring and synthesizing knowledge and using it to develop understanding. The scholar finds bliss in occupations which other dispositions would find too withdrawn and under-stimulating. Thomas Aquinas spending years in his library, conceiving and writing arcane texts while striving to reconcile Christian theology with Aristotelian philosophy, is an example of a scholar disposition in action.

In music, where an artisan would be more likely to seek bliss in the perfect performance, a scholar would be drawn towards discovering the perfect composition. This is not to say that artisans do not compose and scholars do not perform. They do, and may be highly successful. But each approaches the tasks of performing or composing differently. A scholar in the arts is more likely to have wider-ranging interests than an artisan, who would focus more on the task of physically manipulating the instruments and the music. Leonardo da Vinci displays a typical scholar disposition in the huge range of his interests.

Scholars provide humanity with concepts. They are naturally inclined to assimilate and process information. They can also be relentless in pursuing new knowledge. They push humanity to move into new intellectual territory, and to adopt new theories, new understanding. Because they tend to be methodical and logical, they see through the posturing, coercion and humbug of others.

The positive manifestation of the scholar disposition is displayed when knowledge is collected and organised to achieve insight and understanding. Scholars also possess a natural dispassion that enables them to detach from physical and emotional circumstances and process what is going on. The negative manifestation of the scholar disposition results in superficial collecting and list-making and a preference for theory rather than practical knowledge. The scholar's natural detachment can also result in emotional coldness and a lack of connection to others.

Examples of scholars: Marcus Aurelius, Leonardo da Vinci, J.S. Bach, Shakespeare, George Fox, Beethoven, Charles Darwin, Mary Shelley, Sigmund Freud, Krishnamurti, Michelle Obama.

SAGE

The sage disposition is the most outward-going of all core dispositions. Sages are natural performers – although not all natural performers are sages, and not all sages are performers. To offer a general statement, sages love putting on a show. Those with a sage disposition are naturally drawn to careers in which communication is central and that offer them the opportunity to strut their stuff. Careers that appeal to sages include entertainment, law, politics and religion. Whether as an actor, comedian, poet, musician, chef, priest, judge, teacher, or barman, sages love an audience. They achieve their bliss through communicating and performing.

But sages need a content to communicate. At the immature end of the communication scale, sages indulge in empty rhetoric, repeating others' material because they have nothing of significance to say from themselves. For immature sages it is all about the saying, and showing off while doing so. At the mature end of the scale, sage performance delves into deep situations, expresses profound emotion, and makes sagacious observations regarding the human condition. Sages are conduits who celebrate shared human experience. They voice what is common to all, but that most are unable to articulate so aptly or powerfully. When they gain personal experience they offer words, music and performance that lift others into higher realms of feeling.

Examples of sages: G. F. Händel, W.A. Mozart, King Louis 14 of France, Puccini, Augustus Caesar and Dag Hammerskjold (same spirit), Franklin Roosevelt, William Faulkner, Lenny Bruce, Whoopi Goldberg, Michael Moore, J.K. Rowling, Oprah Winfrey.

PRIEST

Those with a priest disposition find their bliss in serving a common ideal and lifting others towards it. As with the servant disposition, those possessing the priest disposition need to choose that ideal for themselves.

The priest disposition offers inspiration. She or he achieves bliss in lifting others into higher states of being. Understandably, in the past this has meant priests served in religions, acting as shaman, initiator, temple priest or healer. As with Oliver Cromwell and Martin Luther King, many priests have sought religious or political power in order to free and uplift their people. Today opportunities for priests to express their innate disposition include teaching, social work, psychology, and healing of all kinds.

Priests are driven by compassion for others. But where servants focus on people, and so the ideal is less important than supporting others, priests are more oriented towards their ideal, and so view others in relation to what may be achieved. This is a subtle but important distinction. Historically, priests have advocated for shared betterment, and both publicly and in their private lives have stimulated the human will to achieve it. Religions throughout history are the work of those possessing the priest disposition.

Of course, there are downsides to religion and to the desire to exhort and inspire others. The negative expression of the priest disposition manifests in being overly zealous and in attempting to force others to believe what they do. This has resulted in religious crusades and the Christian Inquisition. Priests may also have a problem controlling the manifestation of their sex drive. When priests engage in indiscriminate or forbidden sexual encounters, while continuing to advocate for the high moral standards, they end up betraying their own ideals.

On the other hand, a positively expressed priest disposition manifests in a human being who is full of compassion, who ignites a spark in others to better themselves, and who is naturally inspiring, uplifting, and offers wise counseling and guidance. Any situation or occupation that gives priests the opportunity to do this will see them achieving their bliss.

Examples of priests: Francisco Goya, Jack the Ripper, St. Frances of Assisi, Oliver Cromwell, Jeanned' Arc, Frédéric Chopin, Napoleon Bonaparte, Gandhi, Helena Blavatsky, Carl Jung, Ayn Rand, Martin Luther King.

KING

Those with a king disposition find their bliss in possessing a kingdom, no matter how large or small, and leading others in it. It may be in politics, in business, in the military, in music, or in common labouring. Wherever kings are, they are only content when they are in a positions of leadership or authority. Of course, it is entirely possible to lead from behind, without others noticing.

If anyone may be said to be a born leader it is those who possess the innate disposition of king. Naturally charismatic, all the other dispositions are happy to follow the king. That is, as long as the king manages opportunities for each of them to follow their bliss. And the king is the individual who is temperamentally equipped to carry out this kind of complex balancing act.

Formulating orders and wielding authority come naturally for kings. The roles of party boss, head of a clan, hotel manager, orchestra conductor, business leader and star actor sit easily with them – although naturally this does not mean that all party bosses, orchestra conductors, business leaders or star actors possess a kingly disposition.

In its positive manifestation, the king disposition leads others to perform to the height of their abilities. The negative manifestation of the king disposition is expressed in a relentless drive to be first, to get the crown and keep it, and to be willing to walk over everyone and everything to win it. The natural leader then becomes an unforgiving and oppressive tyrant who forces others to conform to his or her will and who punishes those who don't.

Examples of kings: Alexander the Great, Cleopatra, Lorenzo de Medici, Niccolo Machiavelli, Elizabeth 1 of England, Igor Stravinsky, Bette Davis,

John F. Kennedy, Thich Nat Hahn, Sean Connery, Cate Blanchett, Donald Trump.

A WARNING

When you initially attempt to apply these seven core dispositions to yourself and to others you know well, you cannot use them as simply as these brief descriptions of their qualities suggest. This is because they do not manifest and play out in the world as straightforwardly as these descriptions suggest.

For example, it cannot be assumed that teachers or clergy who use their positions to molest children necessarily have a core disposition of priests and are struggling to manage their sexual energy. That may be the case. But it may equally not be. Other factors also generate the same behaviours. Equally, just because individuals love books and libraries doesn't mean they have a scholar core disposition. Parental upbringing, which influences the development of the social self, may be responsible.

The key question to ask when seeking to identify another's core disposition is: what is that person's bliss? This question is not always easy to answer due to the layers of socialisation and conditioning, behaviours generated by the body, and deeper essence drives, all of which overlap and mitigate how individuals manifest their deepest impulses.

In addition, two further factors at the level of the spiritual self also impact significantly on the way that the core disposition manifests during its life journey. These factors are modality and secondary disposition.

CHAPTER 3

Modality and Secondary Disposition

HAVING JUST PRESENTED A MODEL outlining the seven core dispositions, the point needs to be made that this model is incorrect. Or, at least, it is limited in its application. The fact is people do not fit so snugly into seven simple categories. Observation indicates that some people are naturally extroverted and others introverted. Some are good with their hands, others are great communicators. Some like to carefully think things through before acting, others are too impatient or lazy to ever consider carefully, and yet others can never make decisions at all. Then there are moments of crisis, which reveal deeper psychological natures. Under pressure, some people collapse while others rise to the challenge. Some leap at opportunities to nurture others, some enjoy commanding, others only want to follow.

The point is, this complex range of human characteristics is not captured in the simple formulation of the seven core dispositions. Human character is too complex, too multilayered, and no simplistic formulation is capable of capturing all that complexity or encompassing everything in the layers.

Of course, this is merely common sense. It is certainly not a surprising statement to anyone who has observed the way that a close friend, or family member, or work colleague, receives the same information as you but responds very differently. You perceive one way, they perceive another. You process information one way, they process the same information in another. The result is divergent decision-making. Or it may perhaps be that you both agree on the same final decision, but your individual decisions are reached using quite different reasoning.

Accordingly, it is a given that simple models cannot adequately capture all the complexities of human behaviour. But this model does indicate something very interesting about how deeply these differences in human perception, processing and decision-making go. Because they go all the way down.

The starting point for the perspective offered here is that human beings are a spirit existing within a body. As a spirit-body identity, individuals express themselves in complex and multilayered ways that incorporate their body, their psychological make-up, their conditioning, and their inherited abilities and talents. But beyond these, individuals also make choices that feel right yet that occur at such a deep level within them that they are hardly conscious of, or even not at all, let alone able to articulate.

As just noted, the spirit's complex and multilayered manner of expression is not easily captured by simplistic formulations. The aim of this book, as with the books in this series, is to explore this complexity in a necessarily simplified way in order to facilitate understanding of the multiple levels of human nature.

MODALITY

The spirit's complex and multilayered expression begins with its core disposition. While each individual spirit fits into one of the core disposition categories of servant, artisan, warrior, scholar, sage, priest and king, in reality not all servants are servants in the same way. Nor are all artisans artisans in the same way. Nor all warriors or all scholars, and so on.

Some spirits, at their very core, are naturally more inclined to be inward. Others are innately more outwardly directed. Some combine inward and outward tendencies. Some lean towards expression, others naturally seek action. Each individual spirit combines these qualities in greater or lesser proportions and percentages. One means of appreciating this difference at the spiritual core is through the concept of modality. Modality mediates the way that each core disposition manifests. At this stage we define three modalities: inward, outward and expressive.

A spirit dominated by the inward modality is naturally more drawn to contemplative modes of processing the experience of living.

A spirit dominated by the outward modality naturally tends towards giving themselves over to participating in life experiences, especially initiating actions.

A spirit dominated by the expressive modality naturally seeks to give outward expression to inward thoughts and feelings.

Of course, modality is not this simple. It is extremely rare for anyone to be wholly inward, outward or expressive. Instead, each individual spirit possesses a combination of the three modalities. For example, at their core two individuals may naturally and equally lean towards the expressive modality. But one may also lean towards the inward modality while the other leans towards the outward modality. This means that the first leans towards expressing subtle inner discoveries, while the other facilitates communication that is focused on outward forms of activity. Nonetheless, the active communicator still has an inward, self-reflective component in their make-up, and the

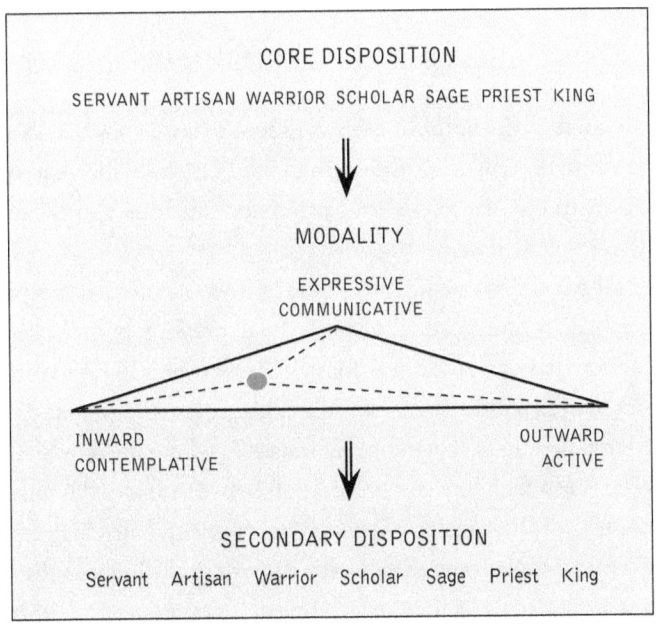

FIGURE 3.1

inward meditator still shares insights in outwardly-directed expression and action.

This balance between the three modalities is visualised in FIGURE 3.1. As can be seen, while one possible position is indicated in the graphic, in practice there are a huge number of different positions whereby an individual core consciousness may be situated within these three points. Different individuals possess different percentages of the contemplative, expressive and action modalities. These variations may be subtle, but they impact on how bliss is achieved.

The degree of bliss individuals achieve in each lifetime depends on the degree to which they are able to give expression to the disposition of their core spiritual consciousness during the course of fulfilling their life plan. Giving their core consciousness expression in turn depends on finding a place in their social and cultural environment that offers opportunities to do so. There are many obstacles to doing this, which we will examine later. For now we need to examine the other significant aspect that impacts on the expression of core consciousness: secondary disposition.

SECONDARY DISPOSITION

Each individual spirit expresses itself via a secondary disposition. Secondary disposition functions as a psychospiritual medium via which the core consciousness manifests. In a sense, it flavours or colours a spirit's manifestations. An example will make this clear.

Let's say a spirit has a core disposition of warrior, and that this particular warrior's modality tends overall towards the expressive, but also leans more towards action than towards inwardness. This warrior is likely to seek bliss in social roles such as politics, social work, teaching, or environments dominated by workshopping and exchanges of information, where the aim is to directly engage others and facilitate communication between them. All this is in the deeper context of the warrior enjoying challenges and striving to persuade others to embrace them too. Secondary disposition influences the way the warrior manifests that specific combination of inner nature and drive.

Accordingly, if the warrior's secondary disposition is scholar, then he or she would naturally inwardly stand back and enjoy synthesising information. If the secondary disposition is sage, the warrior would be something of a natural performer and all actions would possess a certain flair. This flair will be pronounced, or quiet and subdued, or full of shades of expression, depending on whether the warrior's overall modality veered more towards outward, inward or expressive.

If the secondary disposition is warrior, then the warrior would naturally possess a powerful momentum which drives him or her to challenge boundaries and to dare to do things that others would faint at even contemplating. It is in this sense that secondary disposition may be thought of as providing any core disposition with a secondary flavour or dye that adds colour to an individual's fundamental make-up.

Secondary disposition manifests more directly when interacting with others, while primary core disposition remains hidden. The result is that if a warrior's secondary disposition is sage, others are much more likely to observe the sage performative characteristics and much less likely to see the deeper warrior drives.

Accordingly, when attempting to observe your own or another's innate nature, be aware that secondary disposition manifests more immediately and clearly. It takes considerable observation and analysis to get under the surface and discover an individual's core nature. Striving to understand what their bliss consists of helps penetrate to that deep level.

CONCLUSION

What the concepts of core disposition, modality and secondary disposition attempt to communicate is the complexity that exists within each individual's spiritual make-up. Far from being either simply good or bad, wise or ignorant, each individual spirit possesses its own unique signature or flavour.

Of course, identifying what precisely this is is difficult. It takes extended observation over time to discern the subtle shades that colour a person's psychospiritual make-up. This is a case when first impressions are not correct, because they can only ever provide a very partial and superficial view of the complex and deep whole.

The key point is not to get caught up in the detail and or in trying to discern who among your family and friends is what combination of core disposition, modality and secondary disposition – although having some insight into those three will certainly facilitate greater understanding of the way they seek their bliss and why they make the decisions they do. Rather, the key point we initially wish you to take away from this chapter is an appreciation that such diversity exists at a core level within the spiritual identity. At their most inward and intimate level, individuals are this complex and diverse!

CHAPTER 4

The Model of
The Five-Layered Self

WHEN A CORE CONSCIOUSNESS enters a human body, and that body is born, a new unique human identity comes into being. This human identity exists for the period of a lifetime, then dissolves when its body dies. However, the experiences the human being undergoes are not lost. They continue to be real for the core consciousness, because after the body dies they are uploaded to the spiritual self for evaluation. The quintessence of what has been experienced is then extracted. It subsequently influences the spirit's ongoing existence and what it chooses for its next incarnation.

In this way a unique human being, which exists for the period of one lifetime, becomes a sub-personality of the ongoing spiritual identity. This sub-personality has validity, derived from its experiences and from what it feels, thinks and does in response to its experiences. During its life the sub-identity is changed by what it experiences. It also changes itself as a result of processing key experiences. It does this by adjusting its behaviour and decision-making based on what it decides is best in current circumstances.

Key experiences that are undergone during any lifetime include moral choices, intellectual endeavour, the sharing of love in myriad ways, curiosity regarding the nature of existence, and enquiring into the origins of what exists and how it came to be. Open engagement in deep feeling, focused action, self-reflection, creative exploration, inner withdrawal – all these give depth and breadth to a life journey and help generate significant life experiences.

Traditionally, religious, philosophic and scientific thought have attempted to capture the complexity of the sub-identity that is generated during the course of a single lifetime by using the conceptual juxtaposition of soul and body or mind and body. However, this basic dichotomy is insufficient to explain the complex psychology and behaviours of human beings. Hereditary, social conditioning, education, accidental influences, and what is involuntarily and voluntarily taken on board, all shape the sub-identity that develops during the course of a lifetime.

Accordingly, it is proposed that a new model for the self be adopted, a model we first proposed in *Experimental Spirituality*. The purpose of this model is to provide a conceptual framework sufficiently complex to facilitate a meaningful exploration of the levels of human identity. This model asserts that human identity is constituted of five layers: the biological self, the socialised self, the essence self, the energetic self and the spiritual self.

THE FIVE LAYERS OF THE SELF

The biological self is the body. It encompasses a set of physiological givens into which human beings are born. These include the senses, the brain and autonomous nervous system, biological urges and drives, and physical characteristics inherited genetically via the individual's parents.

The socialised self channels biological drives, modifying them into socially acceptable behaviours. For example, the biological urge to satisfy hunger and thirst is socialised into preferred foods and drinks and using certain eating utensils and manners; the sexual urge is socialised into marriage; the urge to find clothing and shelter is socialised into obtaining paid employment to pay for them; and the biological urge to claim territory is socialised into taking out a mortgage on a house.

Human beings together live in shared physical and cultural environments. Accordingly, the biological and socialised selves dominate daily existence. However, the biological self is limited to human animal functioning, while the socialised self is entirely the result of cultural conditioning. The higher capacities that shape human existence, including complex emotional responses and the ability to think abstractly, derive from a deeper level of the layered self, the essence self. The essence self divides into three primary capacities: moving, emotional and intellectual. The moving capacity encapsulates motor skills, the emotional capacity consists of complex emotional responses, and intellectual capacity encompasses thinking.

It must be noted that these three areas of the essence self overlap with the biological self. This is because without the nervous and limbic systems and the brain's cognitive capacities human beings wouldn't be able to move, feel and think as complexly as they do. Nonetheless, essence qualities are not identical with physical abilities: painting the wall of a house is of a significantly different order of accomplishment to painting the Sistine Chapel, even though both use the same motor skills of applying paint to a surface. The difference is in the essence qualities of emotion, thought and movement that manipulate form and colour, and that generate the story-telling that underpins the figures depicted in the Sistine Chapel.

Essence qualities are perfectly capable of being developed during the course of a lifetime. Indeed, that is a point of possessing them. Human beings use them to learn. Each person is born with certain innate essence level propensities and talents inherited via parental genes. But these can be extended when engaged and pushed towards the upper limits of their capacity.

MODEL: THE FIVE LEVELS OF THE LAYERED SELF

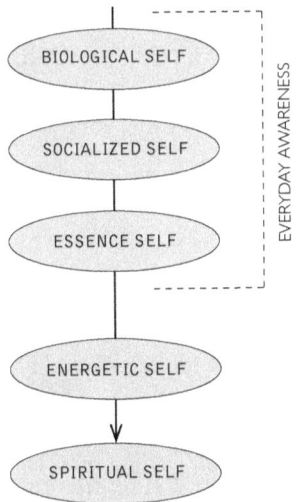

FIGURE 4.1

The result is that anyone can perfect their essence level skills, expand their essence abilities, and direct their essence talents into new areas of accomplishment. It is in the essence self that each individual matures into a more accomplished, more rounded, and deeper human being. It is on that level that each human identity blooms.

The energetic self is a special construct that functions as a bridge between the spiritual and physical domains. It is known traditionally as the aura, but its function is more complex than this term allows. It both shapes physical structures and enables communication to occur between the physical and spiritual levels.

The spiritual self, also termed here core consciousness, is the identity that existed before the body was born. It underpins human identity, which is really a sub-identity of the ongoing spiritual self. Sub-identities are born, grow, mature and die during the course of a lifetime. On its body's death the spiritual self withdraws its connection from that body and its sub-identity, which dies along with body. The spiritual self then processes what has been experienced, developed and learned, using it as part of its preparation for choosing its next body and sub-identity.

The final key concept derived from this model of the five-layered self is that of everyday awareness.

EVERYDAY AWARENESS

Everyday awareness consists of the combined manifestations of the layered self's active aspects. In general, all five layers are not active together. That is, they do not contribute an equally active component to any sub-identity's awareness as it engages in the tasks of daily life.

In practical terms, the biological self and the socialised self are automatically engaged and active during the course of daily living, while the essence self is actively engaged only to the extent that a human being draws on that level's capacities. This means that all of the moving, emotional and intellectual capacities are not automatically or equally utilised in daily life. Essence level capacities only manifest to the extent that the individual consciously draws on them.

Finally, most individuals scarcely consciously engage with their energetic and spiritual selves at all. These selves remain present and functioning, but they are passively present. This passive presence may be understood by comparing it to the functioning of the autonomous nervous system within the body, that being the part of the biological self that is responsible for breathing, digestion, controlling core body temperature and for sending chemicals and enzymes around the body in order to keep it alert and functioning. The everyday awareness of the awake human being is not conscious at all of the autonomous nervous system's functioning. Yet that doesn't inhibit the nervous system from doing what it does in order to keep the body working and the human animal alive. In exactly the same way, the energetic and spiritual selves are present in each human being, doing what they do to keep the individual alive and functioning, but without the individual being aware of them. Of course, this does not preclude occasions when the individual becomes temporarily aware of, and consciously engages with, the energetic and spiritual layers of its own self. It is just that during the course of everyday living these two levels do not have a permanent, let alone a consistently intermittent, presence in the individual awareness.

Hence, everyday awareness may be defined as involving those parts of the five-layered self that are actively used in daily life. These layers tend overwhelmingly to involve just the body, the socialised self and those aspects of the essence self that the individual consciously utilises.

This means that when an individual engages with the deeper, unused parts of the essence self, and when it engages with its own energetic and spiritual layers, these engagements occur in short or extended periods of heightened awareness. Obviously, heightened awareness, as a state, is distinct from everyday awareness. States of heightened awareness may occur as an accidental by-product of situations that generate huge stress or trauma. They may also be consciously generated through concentration, such as focused listening to music, reading, appreciating arts or engaging in creative activities of all kinds. Meditation, prayer, yoga and martial arts are long proven activities that generate heightened states of awareness.

Obviously, only a few individuals incorporate these activities into their daily routines. But the level of everyday awareness, that is, the depth incorporated into any person's everyday awareness, may be increased by consciously engaging in activities that generate heightened awareness. And the longer they are engaged in, the higher and deeper everyday awareness becomes.

EVERYDAY IDENTITY

Everyday identity is a function of those aspects of the whole self that are actively engaged during everyday living. To the extent that what individuals identify with within their layered self changes during the course of each day, everyday awareness may be said to be fluid. As a result, everyday identity may be said to be constantly shifting.

For example, let's say a man is a parent. Each morning, on waking, he is a father. This father plays out the social role of parenthood, which role is itself derived from the biological self having physically reproduced with his partner. He performs his social role of parent according to a range of parameters, which include conditioning regarding what the role of parent should be, indifference to that conditioning, or even rejection of it. His upbringing also influences the way he performs the role of parent, with modelling by his own parents, personal childhood pleasures and traumas, and his particular psychological make-up all impacting on how he fulfils his parenting role.

Let's follow the father. Let's say he drops the children at school then drives on to work. For a period he is a frustrated commuter as he sits for what feels like an unnecessarily long time in traffic cues. Depending on his emotional state, he may respond in a helpful or angry way to the behaviour of other drivers, assisting or impeding their progress. He then arrives at work.

Now his social role changes to worker, shopkeeper, manager, boss, chairman, contractor or whatever other employment role he engages in to earn an income. Within the activity of employment there may be several roles he performs in a day. He may be required to oversee others for a period, and so become a manager, or be required to show others what to do for a time and so become a teacher, or be required to justify a line of expenditure to a senior manager and so become a subservient worker following orders.

After work he may stop to have a drink with friends and colleagues. He tells stories about his day, hears their stories about their day, and tells jokes, vents frustrations, or exaggerates problems or successes. One friend may have a problem so they go off and talk privately for a time. Thus he becomes a confidante and perhaps advisor. He then returns home where he once again becomes a father to his children and partner to his significant other.

During this one day he has lived in a range of social roles, including spouse, parent, commuter, manager, teacher, underling, and friend. Each role draws on different aspects of his psychological make-up. For example, he may be short with his children but very patient when showing a work colleague how to do a task. Or visa versa. All this depends on the interplay of his particular psychological traits.

The upshot is that his everyday awareness changes with each role. Why? Because performing each requires that slightly different parts and traits of the socialised and essence selves be brought into play. One role may require practical thinking. Another role may require emotional sensitivity. And another intellectual engagement. So the quality of the everyday awareness changes from one state to another, as required in order to satisfactorily perform the role.

With these changes in everyday awareness everyday identity also changes. This is not a difficult concept to grasp. Each individual, every day, moves quite naturally, unthinkingly even, between the roles of partner, parent, commuter, worker, teacher, friend, confidante. What few consider is that as they engage in each role, so their identity shifts. They manifest a slightly different, or even a significantly different, identity in each role.

In this sense everyday identity changes a little or a great deal as individuals shift from one role to performing another. Some individuals are comfortable and happy at home with their family, but feel downtrodden, under-used, frustrated or exploited at work. Others are relaxed at work but a tyrant at home. For some their everyday identity is integrated, with little change in inner feelings and external behaviour as they shift between their different roles, while for others there is a great diversity of psychological states across their roles, and so their everyday identity swings between extremes. Accordingly, as everyday awareness subtly or demonically changes in order to perform different social roles, so does everyday identity – which is what people feel themselves to be – alter with it.

As a side note, it can be seen that all social roles are grounded in biological necessity. The role of parent is a socialisation of biological reproduction, while the task of earning money, with the wide range of social roles and relations that it engenders, is to provide food and shelter for the family's bodies. Friendship arises, in many cases, out of relationships stimulated by parenthood and work, although shared interests and hobbies, which may be connected to neither, also bring people together.

The arising of everyday identity leads to the concept of non-everyday identity.

NON-EVERYDAY IDENTITY

Just as everyday identity arises and changes as a consequence of everyday awareness shifting to perform social roles, so non-everyday identity becomes apparent as a consequence of shifts in awareness into heightened non-everyday states.

As individuals experience these non-everyday states, so they begin to sense that their identity expands beyond the relentlessly physical and social limits imposed on their awareness by everyday living. They come to experience, appreciate and understand the unlimited nature of their non-everyday spiritual self. Especially, they come to realise the *fact* that their identity, as opposed to their *sense* of their identity, is so much greater than what they experience while their awareness is fully identified with, and constrained by, the physical body and social role-playing that results when human beings live together.

THE ESSENCE SELF

The essence self is the key to individuals expanding their functioning daily capacities, and to expanding their sense of personal identity beyond the social, and eventually into the spiritual.

The essence self is where individuals learn. It is what they use to develop skills, nurture abilities and express their talents. The essence self is where human beings grow. Activities involving moving tasks and practical problem-solving, emotional engagement, and intellectual inquisitiveness and ordering, all originate in the essence self. It is these essence-level moving, emotional and intellectual capacities that make human beings human.

The body's nervous system and its brain allow for complex functioning, which facilitates the perception and processing of subtle sensory experiences. These in turn feed the essence self. So the essence self is grounded in the body's biological mechanism.

The essence self also necessarily expresses itself via social envirnonments. Without other human beings to interact with, the essence self, no matter how full of potential functionality, would be silent. The essence self needs the input provided by social environments to draw on and grow, and it needs those same social environments to express itself to other human beings.

Accordingly, in order to appreciate how a spirit expresses itself during the course of a lifetime, it is necessary to look in more detail at each of the essence and socialised selves. We will do that in the next two chapters.

CHAPTER 5

The Essence Self

EACH TIME A SPIRIT ENTERS A BODY, it becomes the core consciousness of a new human being. From a spiritual perspective, we can say that each new human being is actually the new sub-identity of an ongoing spiritual identity. Each of a spirit's sub-identities has a unique personality that is shaped by conditions prevailing in the physical environment, by social conditioning, by inherited traits, and by the way the individual responds to life experiences. The model of the five-layered self is an attempt to capture the complexity involved in shaping each new individual personality.

The biological self is a given over which the individual, once he or she is born into it, has little control. By this we mean that individuals cannot change their body type, basic musculature, genetic make-up, and so on. Of course, they do have the choice as to whether or not to look after their biological self. Yet sometimes, due to famine, war, economic situation or social oppression, even that choice is not available. As these things cannot be altered, the biological self can be treated as a given.

The socialised self, which is shaped by social conditioning and by the possibilities present in the social environment, is largely shaped by external factors. Individuals have no control over the language, cultural outlook, social mores and normative behaviours of the community into which they are born. However, there may be possibilities for altering them to some extent, particularly by moving into different social environment.

The socialised self is largely shaped during childhood years by conditioning and by the way the individual reacts to nurturing and traumatic experiences. In adulthood, the socialised self exists largely as a negotiated equilibrium between inner drives and desires and what is permitted by the social environment. In this sense, the socialised self may be largely viewed as a given.

This leaves the essence self as the key part of the five-layered self that reflects an individual's choices, effort and talents. It plays a crucial role in the choices the sub-identity makes during the course of its life journey, and in the way it draws on its own innate abilities, skills and talents. It is in the essence self that the individual becomes a unique human identity.

THE NINE PARTS OF THE THREE CENTRES

The essence self consists of the three moving, emotional and intellectual centres. They are called centres because each is the centre of a range of perceptions and ways of responding to sensory input and for processing information. Three points need to be made about the centres. First, each centre functions independently of the other two. Second, each individual has a natural predilection for one of the three centres over the other two. And third, the functions of the three centres overlap, resulting in nine parts.

With respect to the first point, movement, emotion and thought are completely different and separate spheres of activity. As a result, the moving, emotional and intellectual capacities function independently of each other. We'll give an example. Let's say you hear a waltz composed by Chopin. Using your moving centre you can respond to the rhythm and physically dance. Using your emotional centre you can feel the emotional power of the melody. And using your intellectual centre you can analyse the score. You could, of course, do all three simultaneously. But this doesn't alter the fact that moving, feeling and thinking are three intrinsically distinct ways of responding to the music.

The second point is that everyone has a natural predilection for one centre over the others. You may prefer the emotions. Or moving and action. Or thought. This doesn't mean you don't use the others, just that you prefer one.

Third, the three centres overlap. They do so by breaking into three sub-functions, each consisting of moving, emotion and thinking. So the moving centre has moving, emotional and intellectual sub-functions, as do the emotional and intellectual centres. This means that the three centres collectively possess nine parts between them. (See FIGURE 5.1)

The impact of this sub-division is not just that human beings' experiences are incredibly enriched. It also means that you don't just have a predilection for the moving centre, you have a predilection for one of the moving, emotional or intellectual parts of the moving centre. This makes each human being one of nine types. Accordingly, if a person prefers the emotional centre, they express their predilection via either the moving, emotional or intellectual part of the emotional centre.

This all sounds complicated. In practice, it is simpler than it seems.

THE MOVING CENTRE

The moving centre manifests in physical movement and expresses itself via motor functions, which provide the moving part of the moving centre. Activities such as walking, changing a tire on the car, playing sports, and building a house, each involve physical movement and so utilise the moving part of the moving centre.

The emotional part of the moving centre manifests in body-focused emotions. Positive moving emotions include the physical joy derived from marching, dancing, playing sport or gardening. The two most common forms

THE NINE PARTS OF THE THREE CENTRES

	MOVING	EMOTIONAL	INTELLECTUAL
MOVING CENTRE	Pure movement	Adrenaline emotions	Common sense
EMOTIONAL CENTRE	Appreciate form	Empathy, love	Intuition
INTELLECTUAL CENTRE	Formatory apparatus	Scale, awe	Pure intellect

FIGURE 5.1

THE ESSENCE SELF

of moving centre emotions are instinctive and adrenal. Instinctive emotions include those involved in mating and nurturing children. Adrenaline emotions are used in sport and physical confrontation. When the instinctive and adrenaline emotions reinforce each other – which they do in territorial and ownership disputes that lead to physical fighting – they become very powerful and potentially destructive.

Everyone experiences instinctive and adrenaline emotions from early childhood. As such, they are common denominator emotions. Instinctive emotions are expressed via familial love and general concern for the young. Adrenaline emotions are socially expressed these days via sports, whether playing or watching, and by using physical force to solve emotional confrontations and problems. Adrenaline emotions are very coarse, and when stimulated they can easily tip into violence, as manifested by hooligan sports fans and domestic violence. If adrenaline emotions were used to dominate or terrorise a child as it grew up, it will either shy from them for the rest of its life or will be acclimatised to using them on others.

The intellect of the moving centre provides common sense, used to think through practical issues and problems. Figuring out how best to attach a hose to a pipe, where a pile of sand should be dumped to facilitate the work ahead, and what cables should be connected to which plugs, are tasks that utilise the intellect of the moving centre. The intellect of the moving centre also has a creative element, which manifests in simple tasks such as drawing up a diagram of how best to arrange wedding guests around tables. The diagrams and plans drawn up by engineers and architects are high-end examples, being abstract and stylised drawings that are applied to practical outcomes. Creative moving centre thinking also applies to activities such as planning events, project managing, town and environmental planning, and to adjusting a plan to reality on the ground.

THE EMOTIONAL CENTRE

Where the moving centre is focused on hands-on activities that involve a pragmatic outcome, the emotions focus on the feelings that are involved while carrying out everyday activities. With respect to the task of digging up the backyard, a moving centred individual would be concerned with what tools were needed and what to do with the fill. An emotion centred individual would be concerned with whether the workers were sufficiently watered and fed, or whether the design fulfilled all the children's needs, or whether the colours and textures of the materials were compatible with the house and its furnishings.

In terms of bodily location, the moving centre is aligned with the spine, whereas the emotional centre radiates from the solar plexus. From there it extends throughout the nervous system, which enables bodily extremities, for example fingertips, to have an emotional content.

The moving part of the emotional centre enables you to appreciate the colours, textures and artistry of the world, and make your own contribution to them. So while the wind moving through the trees is a pure moving activity, the emotional centre interprets the sound the wind makes in the trees as sighing or crying. Similarly, you may have powerful emotional responses to vast and beautiful landscapes and to sunsets. This is because the moving part of emotional centre responds to the textures, power and artistry of the natural world. Appreciation of colours, of objects' textural surfaces, and admiration for the skills and artistry of painters, sculptors, weavers, builders and musicians, emanates from this part.

The emotional part of the emotional centre is where pure emotions occur. It enables you not just to experience the world emotionally but also to enter into the feelings of others. So, on the one hand, emotions as a whole are highly subjective, colouring how you personally experience what occurs in the world around you and hence may be thought of as self-centred. On the other hand, these pure emotions provide you with the means to empathise with others and to feel your way into how they experience the world. Of course, you can only empathise if you first climb out of your total immersion in our own emotional responses.

Pure emotions may be positive or negative. Positive emotions include love, compassion, gratitude and the ecstatic emotional states that mystics experience. Examples of negative emotions include self-pity, anxiety, melancholy and despair.

The intellectual aspect of the emotional brain manifests as intuition.

Intuition makes connections. But where the moving centre intellect connects practical aspects of life, the emotional centre intellect makes connections between the emotional, psychological and artistic aspects of human life. Intuition usually occurs in the form of spontaneous flashes of insight. For example, you may be trying to understand why another person is reacting emotionally in the way they are. You may then remember a particular incident, and in a flash you see into what they are feeling and the feeling's cause.

The embodiment of perceptions into metaphors and symbols is also a manifestation of the emotional centre's intellect. This includes the myths of all civilisations. The symbols created by the intellect of the moving centre refer to practical situations, as on a plumbing diagram. In contrast, symbols created by the intellect of the emotions are attempts to embody intuitions and so need to be interpreted emotionally. If the intellects of the moving or intellectual centres are used to decipher the symbols and myths created by the emotional centre, those symbols and myths will appear to be irrational and silly fairy tales. But when processed intuitively they are full of feeling and meaning. The symbols created by the intellects of all three centres are equally meaningful. They're just meaningful in different ways.

THE INTELLECTUAL CENTRE

The moving part of the intellectual brain is an organiser. It enables you to organise and categorise ideas, as well as to compare. In keeping with the impetus of the moving centre, this part is focused on what happens in the physical world.

A useful name for this part is formatory apparatus, due to the way it formally organises information. One of the most common uses of the formatory apparatus is in dividing objects, creatures and people into categories and using those categories to generate lists. A common example is a shopping list. More complex examples include biologists' categorizations of living creatures into a tree of life and John Dewey's decimal system for categorising library books. Academia utilises formatory thinking to compare texts and situate them into historical and conceptual frameworks.

Rule-making, and making sure people keep to the rules, is another activity that uses the formatory apparatus. Bureaucracy revels in the application of the formatory apparatus, often to the exclusion of any other form of thinking, including the emotional centre's intuitive feeling for one's fellow beings and the moving centre's common sense. Religious thinkers have used the formatory apparatus to devise lists of moral do's and don'ts. When applied vigorously, lists created via the formatory apparatus facilitate social control.

The emotional part of the intellectual centre manifests in the way human beings respond to the sight of stars in the night sky with awe, and wonder at powerful and beautiful landscapes. An appreciation of scale is behind awe, giving rise to the realization of how tiny human beings are in the world and the universe. Scale in turn fosters the concept of hierarchy, of one thing being greater or smaller than another, which leads to the emotion of humility.

The intellect of the intellectual centre manifests in humanity's most abstract forms of thinking. This category of thinking seeks to identify patterns in the world, whether these patterns be sub-atomic, biological, philosophic, artistic, theological, mechanical, electrical or cosmological in nature.

The ability to look beyond the material surface of reality, and find abstract connections between elements in it, has led to many of humanity's advances in understanding the way the world operates and manipulate objects and states. From Pythagoras' insight that number underpins the physical world, to Copernicus' insight that human beings live in a heliocentric solar system, to Darwin's theory of evolution, to Einstein's theory of relativity, to quantum physics, to systems theory, abstract thinking has transformed how human beings conceive of reality and pragmatically live today. This is where the power of abstract thinking lies. It is not just in the intellectual overviews it creates, but that it offers new ways to accomplish tasks in the world, tasks that previously hadn't even been conceived as existing, let alone possible.

We observed that these nine sub-functions of the three centres provide a way to think of individuals as essence types. By observing your own innate preferences, and comparing them to the nine sub-categories, you can understand if you are an emotional type with a preference for the moving capacity, that is, a moving-emotional type, or one of the other eight possibilities. We leave you to explore the implications of this abstract framework for yourself.

ESSENCE IS AN EXPRESSION OF SPIRIT

You are wholly responsible for the nature and state of your essence self. It is your creation, resulting from your efforts, choices, preferences and predilections. Before incarnating, you selected which of a range of possible traits and innate abilities you wished to draw on and explore. And during this life you use them, or underuse them, or misuse them, or ignore them, as you see fit. It is entirely your choice.

Accordingly, it needs to be understood that the nature of the essence self you have been born into is not an accident. It is what you have chosen. However, that choice does occur in the context of the sub-identities you have developed during previous incarnations, and it is open or limited according to the essence qualities you have previously worked on. This means you can't choose to be a Mozart or a Madam Curie. You can't leap from limited competence to mastery in one swoop. You need to work towards accomplishment. What you *can* do is select a sequence of essence selves over a series of lives to gradually work towards and achieve mastery in a particular area of expertise. Indeed, that is the whole point of incarnating as a human being. The contribution made to the essence self made by qualities you have developed in prior lives is examined in more detail in Part Two.

For now it is sufficient to note that each consecutive essence self is a manifestation chosen so a spirit may explore certain aspects of human identity and specific areas of the human domain. The purpose is to develop abilities in those areas and eventually to achieve mastery in them. This is made possible through the spirit adopting an essence self that has specific abilities, predilections and talents, and selecting to live in a social environment that facilitates the further development of those traits.

CHAPTER 6

The Socialised Self

EACH SPIRIT EXPERIENCES A LIFE JOURNEY that begins at birth and ends when the body dies. Much happens during the course of a life. Some things are out of an individual's control: natural disasters, war, economic crashes. Some events are chosen: marriage, career, partners of all kinds, special interests. And others are structured into the journey itself: birth, physically maturing from infant to adult, biological urges, illness and death.

We have just looked at the essence self as the spirit's vehicle for experiencing and exploring human existence. Mastery of essence level skills and talents occurs in the context of particular social environments. However, social environments also foster the coming into existence of the socialised self, which impacts significantly on how the essence self is able to express itself.

The socialised self is a negotiation between a spirit's essence self and the social environment in which the individual lives. As noted earlier, everyday identity is fluid, reflecting the involvement of everyday awareness as it shifts between social roles. In contrast, the socialised self is much more fixed. It encompasses the range of social roles between which an individual's everyday identity shifts. It is a crystallisation of a specific range of behaviours, attitudes and emotions. These give coherence to the everyday identity and limit how far it shifts.

Once a spirit selects a particular body, and that body is born, it emerges into a social environment that is not within its control. During the infant's formative years, when the central nervous system and brain of the spirit's new body are developing, it has no ability to control the body in which it

THE SOCIALISED SELF

resides. All the spirit can do is ride out the experience as best it can until the emerging sub-personality is sufficiently mature to make its own decisions regarding what it will and will not do, feel and think. Everything the sub-identity experiences during the course of physically growing and socially maturing impacts on it indelibly and crucially. These impacts cannot be undone. By the age of twenty-one, the nominative age of human maturity, the socialised self has crystallised into a rigid identity. What is crystallised are the psychological traits and behavioural coping strategies that it embraced in response to the impacts of family, community and culture while growing up.

For most individuals, the crystallised socialised self provides their identity for the rest of their lives. When the socialised self possesses crystallised psychological traits that promote essence level growth, this is a positive outcome. But where the socialised self's crystallised traits inhibit essence growth, it is a negative outcome. Most individuals have a socialised self that possesses crystallised nurturing and inhibiting traits.

Crystallised traits that are useful to the essence self as it seeks to maximise its opportunities include acceptance of the need to work hard and the attitude of being open to new ideas. Many crystallised traits are neutral in relation to essence growth, such as tastes in music or clothing. And some are decidedly malicious in the way they are destructive, such as low self esteem and fear of not doing what is expected.

Accordingly, understanding the nature of the socialised self is crucial to making best use of a life's opportunities. Because the socialised self forms in response to the social environment, we'll begin by examining its development.

BIRTH TO TWO YEARS OLD

Each life begins when a spirit enters the body it will "wear" for the duration of that particular life. (There are exceptions, but they are beyond the scope of this discussion.) Developmental psychologists consider it takes around two years for infants to develop a sense of individuality. In the terms being discussed here, we would say that it takes two years before the new sub-personality an individual spirit will project this time round begins to form and manifest.

The two year old's emerging sense of individuality is centred in the socialised self, which starts developing immediately after birth, when the infant begins interacting with others. Touch, gestures and voice tone generate cues that start the process of socialisation. Learning proceeds through imitation. Socialisation proceeds through rejection and approval. Behaviours that are rejected or approved become reinforced in the developing psychological makeup of the emerging personality. Traits of the essence self are present during this emergence, but largely in latent form, with initially only essence-level motor and instinctive functions engaged.

Because human infants are dependent on their parents for survival, family environment provides the key influence in the shaping of the socialised self. This influence lasts well beyond adulthood, often shaping the entire life. The reinforcement of behaviour is key. Human beings are social animals, so they need to interact with others. For the developing baby, interaction involves seeking approval and testing the limits of approved behaviour.

Physically, brain development is crucial to the emergence of a fully functioning personality. Family and physical and social environments are also crucial, because poor nutrition, trauma, and debilitating or abusive physical or home conditions inhibit brain development and potentially distort the development of emerging personality.

The big issue with these first two years is whether satisfactory nutrition, nurturing and stimulus lead to a healthy developing personality, or whether lack of them, or negative stimulus, generates psychological obstacles that will need to be overcome later.

DEVELOPMENT OF CHILDHOOD COPING BEHAVIOURS

The years from two to twenty-one provide the principal developmental period of interpersonal social skills for all human beings. During childhood the individual learns how to cope with life in its family and community. In particular, it develops behavioural mechanisms that enable it to cope with family and local social environments.

Undeniably, there is a dark side to human interaction. Parents have their own behavioural foibles and flaws, as do members of the wider family and those in the local community. Many of these people have the opportunity to influence the growing child in positive or negative ways. Trauma is more frequent than human beings like to admit, with rejection, violence, molestation and general psychological oppression, as well as nutritional trauma in the form of inadequate food, impacting on the child in such ways that he or she develops protective coping mechanisms in order to get through these years.

By adulthood, when the socialised self is crystallised and, for most people, forms the basis of their everyday identity, these coping mechanisms have become habitual and automatically drive responses and decision-making.

Coping mechanisms are forms of behaviour that enable an individual to stabilise itself psychologically when it feels it is approached negatively or attacked in some way. The re-stabilisation involves four principal modes of behaviour: denying, justifying, deflecting and attacking. These manifest in a many different ways, both internally in the form of thinking and emotional reactions, and externally in terms of manifested behaviours. A key to these coping mechanisms is self-calming.

DENYING, JUSTIFYING, DEFLECTING, ATTACKING

When a child (or an adult, for that matter) is upset for whatever reason, it seeks to calm itself by re-establishing its previous inner equilibrium. This is where the defensive behaviours of denying, justifying, deflecting and attacking come in. They help the individual shrug off the perceived threat and re-stabilise internally. These four defensive behaviours manifest in all kinds of situations, at all levels of human interaction, from the personal and one-on-one to the press releases published by major corporations.

Denying involves outright denial of the facts. This currently occurs publicly in discussions of climate change. There is also passive denial, when people deliberately don't hear information or forget what they have been told. Putting one's hands over one's ears is a physical manifestation of denying.

Justifying occurs when an individual admits a point or behaviour, but offers a justification for why it has to be that way. Politicians and business people commonly hide behind the law to justify why they made a decision that impacts negatively on others or that other people consider unethical.

Children engage in deflecting when they try to blame another child for what they have done. Deflecting is often paired with justification, as when an individual justifies what they have done by saying that everyone else is doing it too, or they claim they were forced to do what they did by others.

Attacking others to defend oneself is a very common human trait. This is seen publicly when the characters of whistleblowers are attacked in an attempt to nullify what they have revealed, or when people defend doing something they know is wrong by attacking someone else for doing worse.

These four re-stabilising defensive behaviours go all the way back to when human beings were Paleolithic hunter-gatherers. When an individual or a group were physically attacked they had to physically fight back in order to survive. When the enemy was fought off or killed, those who had been attacked could return to living peacefully, their life re-stabilised. Today attacks tend mostly to be verbal and emotional rather than physical. At the same time socialisation has largely eliminated physical fighting as a permitted response to being emotionally attacked, although of course physical assault still occurs. For the vast majority of individuals, the ancient physical fight or flight mechanism has been socialised into denying, justifying, deflecting and verbally attacking.

TRAUMA AND DESIRES

After a single attack an individual usually automatically re-stabilises and returns to a calm state. However, if the attack is traumatic the shock may go so deep that the individual takes a very long time to re-stabilise. And if shocks and attacks are repeated over an extended period, especially while growing up, the individual's inner state may become so distended that it becomes impossible for them to return to their earlier inner equilibrium. These individuals deal with the consequences for the rest of their lives, struggling to live a comparatively normal human existence.

The majority of the coping mechanisms that growing child develop are in relation to negative impacts, large and small. Sometimes an apparently small incident has an impact out of all proportion to the actual incident. And when small shocks are repeated over time, they may become as significant as a one-off major trauma. Verbal put-downs, anxieties picked up from parents or projected by peers, feelings of inadequacy generated by family, friends, teachers and people in authority, and the cornucopia of fears stirred up by human coexistence, all potentially contribute to defensive behaviours that coagulate into coping mechanisms and then shape the growing personality.

These are inward, reactive components that contribute to the development of the socialised self. But there are also outwardly directed factors. These are embodied in individual's desires. As the growing child seeks to satisfy its desires, it is either successful or thwarted. These outcomes then either reinforce or inhibit those desires. When the same results are repeated over time, they shape the types of desires individuals pursue and the ways they seek to satisfy them in later years.

All parts of the layered self generate desires. From the body come instinctual desires, for food, shelter and sex. From the socialised self come emotional desires to interact, to participate, to be comforted, to comfort, and to be immersed in social experience. From the essence self comes the desire to puzzle things over, manipulate objects and situations, figure out how things work, to make them work better, and to interact more effectively with others. Desires also emanate from the spiritual self, such as the desire to engage with deeper reality beyond the physical and social, and the desire to understand the nature of one's life.

A key contributor to the socialised self's behaviour is sexuality. An individual's sexuality is shaped and defined during the early years, especially with respect to the ways sexuality is expressed – or, should we say, permitted to be expressed. Some cultures prohibit many forms of sexual behaviour, others prohibit them but then turn a blind eye to so-called non-permitted sexuality, and other cultures are very open. In addition, a child's first sexual experiences are frequently formative. For some, fetishes, preferred forms of stimulus, and favourite practices are established during the pre-teen years.

All cultures socialise sexuality, along with the children that result from sex, into approved relationships. Given the layers of inhibition and prohibition around sex – including the Western use of sexuality to sell products, the sexualisation of pre-teen children, the leering, the tut-tutting, and the outright hypocrisy that surrounds sexual expression – human sexuality is a complex and often nefarious activity that frequently generates self-doubt, fear, personal dissatisfaction, jealousy, envy and unhappiness. All these shape the socialised self.

Then there is the balance that is achieved between essence traits and their expression in the world, which for each individual requires they use their socialised self.

THE ESSENCE SELF EXPRESSED SOCIALLY

One of the most significant aspects of a child's development is the psychological task of negotiating a balance between the drives of the essence self and the operations of the socialised self. This negotiation occurs by degrees. It is completed by around eighteen years of age. Developmentally, the moving centre is engaged first, from birth. From seven to fourteen years the emotional centre engages, and from around fourteen to twenty-one the intellectual centre, although individual development does vary.

All emerging essence qualities require a supportive social environment in which to blossom. An individual's social environment may, or may not, be supportive. It depends on what kinds of opportunities are available and whether the social environment itself is conducive to nurturing the particular traits the individual possesses. So the degree to which the essence self is embedded in and is expressed through the socialised self depends on the degree to which external social conditions are inhibiting, encouraging or neutral.

For example, children may have a natural ability in a sport, or for drawing, for making music, for manipulating numbers, for mechanics, or for any other specialised activity. Such abilities reflect innate essence talents. However, these essence traits need to be expressed via a social environment. They blossom in accordance with what is available and possible in the social environment in which they are raised.

If a child has a natural bent for mechanics, but there are no engines, mechanical devices or appropriate toys in the family home, then that talent has minimal early possibilities for expression. A family may even forbid the child from engaging with and expressing a powerful essence talent. The result in such a case is an individual who has a gnawing sense of dissatisfaction or non-fulfilment, the cause of which the individual may or may not be aware, and which may only be resolved in adulthood, if at all.

On the other hand, if the mechanically oriented child is born into a family of builders, or of racing car enthusiasts, family conditions are optimal for nurturing that particular essence trait. Often an individual embarks on a career that is in sync with their predominant essence trait. In such a case, the essence self's expression becomes firmly embedded in, and expressed via, the socialised self. If that trait is also a manifestation of core disposition, bliss will likely be achieved during that life.

If the family environment is not conducive to the expression of essence traits, they may still emerge during schooling where the normal flow of course work or extra-curricular activities provides opportunities for them to be engaged. Alternatively, a teacher may recognise a child's talent and encourage it. As the child's self-confidence grows, and it seeks interactions with those outside the immediate family circle, even more opportunities become available in the wider community for essence traits to be expressed and subsequently embedded into the developing socialised self's traits.

As far as essence engagement is concerned, by adulthood the essence self's moving, emotional and intellectual traits, abilities and talents are largely expressing themselves to the extent that they will for the remainder of that lifetime. The result personality will have achieved a balance between, on the one hand, the essence self's expression of dominant traits and, on the other hand, the socialised self's channelling of that expression. This is a negotiated balance that, whether individuals are aware of it or not, occurs during their childhood years. By the age of twenty-one the negotiation is largely at an end (although for many it is completed earlier than this) and a working balance is crystallised between the expression of the essence self and the way the active parts of the essence self are channelled by the socialised self. The resulting crystallised balance may be satisfactory or unsatisfactory to the essence self. But it effectively becomes the individual's collection of primary everyday behaviours for the rest of that individual's life.

That crystallisation of attitudes, traits and behaviours provides the basis for the individual's everyday awareness and its accompanying identity. This brings us to the question of identity.

THE MAKE-UP OF EVERYDAY IDENTITY

An individual's identity is complex. There are many kinds of identity that reflect the different layers of the human being.

There is the identity of the spiritual self. The spiritual self is an ongoing fragment of consciousness that gives part of itself to form the core consciousness of a five-layered human being. The spiritual self's identity is keyed beyond the physical, in the non-embodied spiritual realm.

There is the identity of the essence self, which embodies those drives and traits that it strives to manifest in this life. One key aspect of its manifestation is defined by its particular balance of moving, emotional and intellectual preferences. Someone is identified as an intellectual, a practical man or woman, or a maternal or paternal type, on the basis of how their essence qualities manifest in what they do.

Next is the identity of the biological self. Most people see this in terms of the body, whether it be beautiful, wiry, plain, sexy, strong, resilient, with lovely eyes, or not, with expressive or delicate or mean mouth, and all the other physical traits that human beings use to approve, reject, worship or ignore others. Yet there are other ways of perceiving bodily identity. Doctors and healers, along with those who use their bodies to generate an income, have quite a different view of the identity of the biological self, based on their knowledge of the body's make-up and the contexts in which they use it. For them, bodily identity is derived from a biological mechanism rather than from likes and dislikes regarding bodily appearances.

Finally, there is the identity of the socialised self, with its outlook, attitudes, conditioning, preferences, judgements, conferred status, and all the accoutrements it puts on and around the body, including clothing, accent, verbal and non-verbal expressions, sexual expression, and so on.

Each of these – spiritual, essence, biological and social – is a layer of the self that, when they are active within everyday awareness, collectively contribute to the make-up of what we can simply term everyday identity. Everyday identity is the identity each human being projects into the world and that everyone else perceives them as being.

However, a complicating issue is that while everyday identity automatically gathers around the crystallised balance between essence traits and the socialised self, in fact identity can grow. It doesn't have to stop growing at the onset of adulthood.

While psychological growth for most people does certainly halt at adulthood, it is possible to undo the crystallisation, give the essence self space to grow, and subsequently generate a new dynamic balance between the essence self and the socialised self. In particular, it is possible to bring the spiritual self into the arrangement. We'll deal with this issue in depth later.

THE SPIRITUAL SELF AND EVERYDAY IDENTITY

For now, and by way of a concluding remark about everyday identity, it needs to be appreciated that each individual human being is a sub-personality, a sub-identity, of their ongoing spiritual consciousness.

This sub-personality, which we are calling everyday identity, results from a spirit's immersion in a body. Everyday identity develops from birth until the period of nominal adulthood, by which time it has crystallised around the socialised self. Unless the individual engages in serious self-reflection, that sub-personality remains unchanged until the body starts degenerating, when the sub-personality begins to break down. It ceases to exist on the physical level when the body dies.

From the widest perspective, each human identity is a sub-identity of an ongoing spiritual fragment. The spiritual fragment adopts a series of human sub-identities as it seeks new opportunities to experience, learn and grow. Any particular sub-identity may be a minor sub-identity in the series. Or it may be a significant sub-identity. Significant in what sense? Significant in terms of the breadth and depth of what it experiences, processes and learns.

The upshot is that any living human identity has behind it a short or long series of previous incarnations. Hence the identity you are now is just a link in the chain, a contributing agent, to a long series of all kinds of sub-personalities via which you, as an ongoing spiritual identity, have experienced human existence in manifold ways. As a result, each human identity is full of subterranean caves, hidden passages, underground streams, roaring torrents, beautiful still caverns, and mysterious places from which whispers and seductive music sound. Though tantalisingly close, these places remain undiscovered and unentered.

What we are calling everyday identity is thus merely one of a substantial collection of sub-identities. The identity that is reading this book has experienced many formative childhood experiences, most of which remain unacknowledged. So it is no surprise that other even deeper identities and influences remain outside your everyday perception.

THE LIMITS OF THE ADULT SOCIALISED IDENTITY

Every human being who reaches adulthood does so with a socialised identity. This identity is needed to interact with others. But the big problem with the socialised self is that it is a conditioned response to childhood experiences. And it is rigid. Both traits inhibit essence growth. In order to grow, it is necessary to crack the crystallised identity that is the socialised self.

Of course, the socialised self exists for this life only. It will dissolve when the body dies, and will be gone. So everyone breaks free of the socialised self at death. Breaking free before death is more problematic.

It is possible to shatter the socialised self's crystallised identity before the body dies. However, the outright shattering of an individual's sense of personal identity is not recommended. It would be so traumatic it would likely kill whoever tried to do so.

Accordingly, rather than shattering the crystallised self, the psycho-spiritual approach is to chip away at the crystallisation, bit by bit, piece by piece. That way, as each part of the crystallised identity drops away, psychological adjustments can be made, old ways of coping changed, long-standing fears dissolved, and a new identity aligned to the spiritual self and its essence self gradually forged.

What stops this piece by piece chipping away at crystallisation? The momentum of everyday identity.

CHAPTER 7

The Momentum of Everyday Identity

HUMAN IDENTITY IS A CONSTRUCT. What is it made of? The actively engaged parts of the layered self. Potentially, all five layers feed into an individual's identity. In practice, for the vast majority of humanity, the socialised drives of the biological self, the active parts of the essence self, and the conditioned socialised self, crystallise to form their everyday identity.

Another way of thinking about crystallised identity is to consider it as possessing momentum. Momentum, by definition, keeps a mass travelling in the same direction at the same speed. Momentum ensures that a moving mass doesn't deviate from its current course. Human everyday identity may be thought of as a mass that, once it is crystallised into its adult form, maintains its same speed and direction throughout the remainder of its life – unless, of course, some huge event alters its course, and allowing that as a body ages its momentum tends to slow, ceasing completely when the body dies.

The everyday identity is constituted of biological drives, essence processes and activities, and socially conditioned attitudes, outlook and behavioural coping mechanisms. All these combine to create a "psychological mass" that causes individuals to move at a particular momentum through life, fending off others by denying, justifying, deflecting or attacking while self-calming in preferred ways, in order to maintain its set speed and direction.

The positive result of the everyday crystallised identity's momentum is that it gives individuals the feeling that they are the same person from one day to the next. The negative result is that momentum keeps an individual travelling along the same narrow inner lanes for years on end, repeating the same thoughts, having the same feelings, and doing the same things. Momentum gives the impression that the individual is moving, that life is changing and developing, that new things are being experienced. But, in fact, the individual is merely travelling down a narrow lane of repeated responses to the same experiences. And no essence growth occurs when the stimulus remains the same and the individual responds with unchanged and repeated thoughts, feelings and actions.

An identity's momentum is sustained by five principle factors. These are: culture, roles, routines, habitual behaviours and conditioned reactions. All five factors additionally fall into the three categories of given, conditioned and chosen. Elements of these three categories play out in each of the five factors that generate the momentum of everyday identity.

CULTURE

Culture is a social given into which a body and the spirit that dwells in it are born. The newly embodied spirit cannot escape culture. Nor should it, for culture provides the context for a spirit to explore the physical and social environments in which it now lives. Each human identity, or to be more exact, each human sub-identity of an ongoing spirit experiencing embodiment, is necessarily born into and grows up in a specific culture.

Cultures are extremely complex. They provide language, world view, social norms, core moral values, socially approved and socially disapproved opportunities for work and play, along with art that projects a notion of shared history and group identity.

The impact of culture on an individual, and equally the degree to which culture shapes identity, cannot be underestimated. Human beings are highly socialised creatures. Culture is imposed on each individual via education. This includes formal state education and informal family and peer input.

That culture is imposed on each human identity is not bad in itself, because a person needs to live somewhere, and imposed culture is unavoidably a part of the package deal of experiencing life as a human being. However, imposed culture is both comforting and disturbing.

Imposed culture is comforting in the way it cocoons an individual and provides it with all the materials it needs to function and grow. It is disturbing in the way that obvious blindnesses, ignorance and even malicious practices are imposed on individuals, which may oppress them physically and psychologically throughout their life. Often imposed cultural inputs, especially those that oppress, limit choices and force individuals to think, feel and act in narrowly regimented ways, impede personal growth. In such circumstances culture becomes a prison that must be escaped.

Because everything that human beings do – work, play, love, pairing, reproduction, raising a family, and essence growth itself – occurs within a cultural context, those who do not view themselves as possessing a spiritual dimension necessarily view their identity as wholly socially constructed. To the degree that they do not consciously allow the impulses emanating from their core consciousness to penetrate into their everyday awareness it may be said that their identity *is* nothing but a social construct. But, of course, human identity is so much more. In fact, the cultures in which individuals live may help them realise they are more than a social construct.

Historically, all cultures have implanted in their citizens religious concepts about how human identity extends beyond the social and physical dimensions. Clearly, some cultures have done this more openly, and with fewer strings attached, than others. Over the aeons some cultures have developed education systems that give more support to essence and spiritual growth than do others. This is where choice comes into play.

Individuals do not have to accept and adopt everything imposed culture projects onto them. During childhood imposed culture conditions people to speak, think, act and feel in certain ways. It shapes social identity, which provides the foundation for everyday identity. But once adulthood is reached, and even before, it is possible to choose which aspects of one's culture one wishes to accept and which one wishes to reject.

In order to exercise choice, individuals first need to analyse their own cultural inputs and appreciate how much of what they think of who, what and how they are is actually a social construct imposed on them, and how much it emanates from their essence self, or deeper. This is a complex and extensive exercise that utilises self-observation. We'll return to this in the next book in this series, *Psychological Spirituality*.

For now it is useful to recognise the degree to which you accept or reject new ideas, such as the ideas presented in this book, is facilitated or hindered by imposed culture, and by your acceptance or rejection of the inhibiting aspects of your imposed culture. For example, many Westerners find the concept of reincarnation difficult to come to terms with. This resistance is largely a reflection of imposed culture. In the West, whether people are brought up a Christian, a Muslim, an atheist, or a scientific materialist, they are brought up to believe that everyone has just one life. But if the same people were born into cultures dominated by the Jain, Hindu or Buddhist religions, the concept of reincarnation would be taught to them from birth by imposed culture.

Of course, there remains the question of what one does with the concept of reincarnation. This is where choice needs to be exercised. Westerners brought up in a one-life cultural perspective have to deconstruct their conditioned assumptions regarding life and death in order to come to grips with the implications of reincarnation. Much will be learned during this process. But other individuals, brought up to believe in reincarnation, may accept it occurs, but do so in a shallow way, without processing what the fact of reincarnation then implies regarding how they should live. So the first begins with incorrect information (the one-life scenario) but eventually achieves understanding, whereas the second begins with correct information (reincarnation) but achieves no understanding.

This means that no matter whether one's culturally imposed beliefs are correct or incorrect, in order to use culturally imposed beliefs to grow and achieve personal understanding they need to be identified, deconstructed, and either rejected or taken on board, then conscious use made of them. In this way imposed and conditioned culture and its beliefs become personally chosen and integrated into an individual's life.

ROLES

Human identity manifests via, and in the context of, social roles. Within any culture an individual is expected to take on a number of established roles and perform them in ways that are socially acceptable. As with culture, in effect these roles are imposed, and in a variety of ways, whether socially, economically, psychologically or legally.

In hunter-gatherer cultures the men had the roles of hunter and warrior while the women's roles primarily consisted of food gatherer, labourer and mother. In contemporary Western culture, with its vaster numbers of people and its greater diversity of opportunities, there are many more roles available, and some choice as to which roles one takes on. As a result, today not all roles are imposed. For example, in a small tribal culture, hunter, father or mother, and family member were the predominant roles. In contemporary Western culture one can reject one's family, decide not to have children, and pursue various social, business, artistic and sporting opportunities.

This means that today there is wider choice than there used to be regarding what roles one takes on. And while some roles are still imposed, there are choices accompanying them. For example, work is an activity required to pay for food and shelter, so the role of worker is imposed. But over time the worker may rise in the business. Consequently, the roles of supervisor, interviewer, instructor, manager, boss, even owner, may become available. In addition, there is choice regarding whether or not a promotion is accepted. Individuals perform well or poorly in each of these roles depending on what innate essence qualities they have to draw on and how motivated they are to perform them well.

Family life naturally has the roles of child, sibling, spouse, parents, grandparents, cousins, and so on. Many play each of these roles during the course of their life. Parents start off caring for their children, and as their bodies decline in health may end up being cared for by their children. Again, how well an individual performs these roles depends on what the individual brings to them and their motivation to do them well.

There is another set of social roles that human beings perform in relation to their friends and peers. These include the larrikin, the coquet, the life of the party, the seducer, the shoulder to cry on, the victim, and the holy terror, each being roles individuals may adopt during social interactions. These roles result from a combination of external and internal inputs.

Coping behaviours adopted during childhood have a significant impact on what kind of social roles individuals adopt. Some children may be small or shy and start telling jokes to hide their feelings of vulnerability and hence become popular with others. So they develop a joker role. A little girl may be pretty, be continually told so by her family, and subsequently realise during her teenage years that she can use her appearance to get what she wants. Depending on other childhood experiences, essence traits, and what she chooses to do with her life, by adulthood she may be a woman who flirts expertly to get her way, a woman who deliberately makes herself look dowdy to avoid attention, or a well-groomed housewife or businesswoman. To cope during an oppressive childhood, an individual may acquiesce and adopt the role of victim, or fight back and adopt the role of crusader, or in adulthood take on the role of oppressor and become a holy terror.

These are generalisations, of course. Our intention is to indicate how roles are imposed, conditioned and chosen, often all at the same time. As with culture, it is necessary that roles be observed, dissected, their contributing circumstances understood, and aspects of roles, or the entire role itself, accepted or rejected in a conscious manner. If this is not done individuals remain imprisoned by their roles, performing them automatically, being pushed involuntarily down the road of life rather than taking charge of the journey and striding towards a chosen destination.

ROUTINES

Daily life is filled with routines such as working, eating, travelling, being entertained, relaxing, sleeping. Repeated routines give lives stability and continuity. Individuals cuddle up to their routines because they become familiar and the familiar generates stability and continuity, which in turn results in a sense of being safe and enfolded in the circumstances of life.

Entire cultures have routines which give daily life its rhythms and pacing. Cultural routines include the working week, annual holidays, public festivities such as Christmas, Eid, Diwali, and Yom Kippur, and shared national observances. Communities have routines that include weekly markets, annual fairs, school holidays and observing shared communal days. Individuals have routines, with birthdays, anniversaries and holidays punctuating the repetition of the working year. All these add flavour to daily life.

The negative aspect of routines is that their repetition leads to individuals always utilising the same parts of their layered self. Naturally, there are exceptions. For example, an annual family birthday get together could stir deeper feelings than normal, and so engage other parts of the socialised and essence selves than is usual. However, this is the exception. Usually, repeated routines lock an individual into a proscribed set of behaviours that draw on the same parts of the layered self.

So the momentum generated by the performance of routines may give rise to imagined stability and continuity, and to the feeling that life is familiar and safe, but the cost is that individuals experience the same things, and feel, think and do the same things, over and over. Drawing on the same parts of themselves, they don't grow. And their identity remains static and partial.

HABITUAL BEHAVIOURS

Habitual behaviours are behaviours that are repeated because they are preferred over others. Turning on the radio or television when you wake in the morning, drinking tea rather than coffee, browsing in certain online stores – all these become habitual behaviours.

Ordinary activities such as smoking, drinking, eating, pursuing sex, avoiding sex, exercising, playing video games, or regularly scratching a specific part of one's body, become habitual behaviour when, after being repeated consistently over a period of time, they become embedded in an individual's routines and are then automatically carried out. Indeed, identity becomes imbued with habitual behaviours to such a degree that a person may become known to others as the person who always plays video games, or knows what is on television, or can rate the latest best-selling romances, and so on.

Habitual behaviours can be positive or negative, opening or inhibiting, freeing or limiting. And they can manifest from any of the human being's five layers. One's core consciousness may have habitual behaviours, such as regular prayer or meditation, or sitting in silence, or listening to music. Similarly, the essence self, socialised self and body each have preferred behaviours – that could equally include sitting in silence, listening to music, or praying – which make it feel good about being in the world. It must also be noted that some individuals enjoy negative and destructive behaviours as avidly as others prefer positive and nurturing behaviours.

There are many ways a human being may interact with the world. There exist a vast range of habitual behaviours. Each individual selects only a small number from the emporium of human behaviour to decorate their existence. And in doing so they utilise only a narrow band of their layered self.

This is the limitation of habitual behaviours. As is the case with routines, they leave one repeating the same behaviours, using the same narrow band of the layered self, doing, feeling and thinking the same things.

The advantage of habitual behaviours derives from how they reinforce activities that enhance inner growth. Having set times in the week when one sits in silence, or studies, relaxes, or plays, are advantageous when they help aspects of the essence self manifest and grow. In this sense, work itself, a routine that reinforces habitual behaviours, can be limiting if it keeps one in the same place within, or liberating if it provides opportunities to challenge oneself, to reflect on one's practices, and to act, feel and think in new ways.

CONDITIONED REACTIONS

Conditioned reactions are emotional responses, attitudes and ideas about the world. They form a part of the defensive behaviours an individual develops during childhood to get through the days. As such, conditioned reactions are a sub-set of all the many coping mechanisms. They originally come into existence as a response to specific incidents. If those incidents are repeated over time, then the conditions reactions manifest automatically.

Conditioned reactions are learned behaviours. Just as Pavlov's dog learnt to salivate every time a bell rang, so human beings learn to react in particular ways every time certain stimuli occur. Racism, sexism and prejudices of all kinds are examples of conditioned reactions. Being brought up in a religion tends to result in believers having conditioned reactions that they automatically fall back on whenever they face complex situations. If an individual is brought up in a sceptical, political, scientific or artistic household, then they will be equally conditioned to respond to daily stimuli in particular ways. The degree to which individuals are aware of their conditioned reactions depends entirely on the extent to which they have examined themselves and considered the ways they automatically react.

Powerful single experiences can also give rise to conditioned reactions. Examples include public humiliation, sexual molestation, and an outstanding success or failure. Given that conditioned reactions may be shaped by single significant experiences, or by small and insignificant experiences repeated over time, they are immensely varied. The rare arrival of a favourite aunt may automatically generate a warm feeling, while someone wearing particular clothing, or using certain words, may do the opposite.

In the public domain, when discussing politics, religion, social values, foreign policy or economics, it is clear how much politicians, demagogues, and the opinionated all fall back on stock phrases and attitudes. It is extremely rare to have a public discussion in which all participants are able to rise above their own conditioned reactions. This is because conditioned reactions dominate most people's thoughts and feelings and lead to automatic rather than considered responses. Given practised individuals have elaborate ways of defending and justifying their conditioned reactions, much of what they feel, think, say or do remains at the level of conditioned reactions.

GENERATING MOMENTUM

During the course of daily living each individual's everyday identity has a momentum that derives from the way they:

(1) respond to imposed culture
(2) switch between proscribed and chosen roles
(3) adopt certain imposed, conditioned and chosen routines along with
(4) habitual behaviours and
(5) manifest conditioned reactions.

These five factors interlock to provide any crystallised everyday identity with the momentum it has during the course of daily life. In a very real sense, the momentum provided by these five factors sweeps up individuals and trundles them through life. They provide a psychological straight-jacket in which the individual lives, and also a lens through which it perceives, experiences and processes the information it collects during its life. Many people find comfort in being so bound up and pushed along. It provides the substance of the life journey they were born to experience. Others are less enthused. Why?

WHY CHANGE MOMENTUM?

Psychospiritually, there is a significant problem with the momentum of everyday identity. The problem is that it resists change. Accordingly, if you wish to see, feel, think and do new things, and particularly if you wish to transform your identity into a spiritualised adult, you need to change your momentum. And to do that you need to disrupt all the cycles of repetition and routine which maintain your daily momentum. But before you can disrupt it you need to understand the nature of your personal daily momentum.

To recapitulate, each human being is a spirit born into a body and a particular social environment. The association between both gives rise to a new sub-identity. During the course of growing to adulthood the sub-identity gains an everyday psychological mass. This mass consists of the socialised drives of the biological self, the behaviours of the socialised self, and the actively engaged parts of the essence self. The sub-identity's interactions with its social environment (through culture, roles, routines, habitual behaviours and conditioned reactions) give the sub-identity the momentum that keeps it functioning day-to-day.

In itself this momentum is not a problem. If during childhood an individual was inculcated with attitudes, values and traits that promote essence growth, then much in the individual's make-up may be limited, but overall they are positive and useful. But this momentum is a problem if it leads to an individual reaching adulthood with negative and self-limiting attitudes, values and traits. Unfortunately, the majority of adults have many negative and self-limiting behaviours, routines and conditioned reactions. Collectively, these inhibit essence growth.

Even for individuals brought up with growth-inducing values and traits, there are always weaknesses and limitations in their psychological make-up that inhibit some aspects of their essence growth. No individual is without negative and limiting psychological traits that inhibit parts of their essence. So everyone needs to change the momentum of their everyday identity. This may be achieved in one of two ways: by changing the social environment in which the crystallised identity lives, or by changing the crystallised identity's psychological make-up.

The first involves individuals shifting into a new set of social circumstances, such as occurs when one changes country for town, town for city, or moves to a different country altogether. This move may involve slight or large changes to one's culture, which in turn impacts on roles and routines. However, this can only ever be a limited or even temporary change. The momentum of everyday identity is so strong that it will seek to re-establish its routines and habitual behaviors. So while new roles may have to be adopted, for example a doctor in the old country may have now to drive a taxi, so changing from boss to service worker, the personality will quickly re-establish its pattern in this situation. Conditioned reactions will likely also remain unchanged. In effect, crystallised identity shifts minimally to adjust to the new social environment, a slightly different equilibrium is established, and then the established momentum of crystallised identity largely carries on as before. For example, when individuals move to a new country they often take their culture, social routines and roles with them, and transplant their language, religion, and lifestyle into their new environment. The outcome is that there is minimal disruption to the momentum of the crystallised everyday identity.

More effective for changing momentum is when individuals change their psychological make-up. In physics, the momentum of a mass can only be changed through the injection of new energy. Similarly, the momentum of everyday identity may only be changed through the introduction of new psychospiritual energy. To do this it is necessary to replace the old energy, which manifests via habitual emotions, thoughts and activities. By adulthood it is this energy, along with the few engaged parts of the layered self, and well-worn pathways between them, that crystallise into the behaviours that embody the momentum of the everyday identity. Accordingly, injecting new energy into the layered self, in order to change momentum, necessarily involves cracking crystallised identity.

We have already noted that shattering crystallised identity is not advised. This is because spirits need their body and their conditioned socialised self as a vehicle. The socialised self is the means by which an individual interacts with others. It is also needed to give expression to essence abilities and talents. Shatter the socialised self and they end up socially naked, with no established means to interact, communicate and grow. Worse, without the grounding in their social environment that the socialised self provides, human beings invariably go mad.

Accordingly, what is needed is a gentle cracking of selected aspects of the crystallised everyday identity. Inner change is most effectively achieved incrementally. One of the keys to starting this process is utilising psychological turning points.

CHANGING MOMENTUM: TURNING POINTS

Momentum is unquestionably a powerful force in people's lives. It gives individuals their sense of continuous identity. And it keeps most individuals moving in the same direction for the whole course of their lives. However, as we have just noted, in order for individuals to grow, to have new experiences and perceptions and to feel and think and behave in new ways, it is necessary to change the momentum of one's life.

For most people, changing momentum involves a confrontation. Confrontation may be either external or internal. External confrontation consists of becoming profoundly unhappy with life circumstances, whether this be with occupation, relationships, marriage, or with an inability to explore interests or express talents. At such times people generally reach a level of such profound frustration or dissatisfaction that they decide a radical change of life circumstances is required.

Internal confrontation involves individuals becoming profoundly unhappy with the way they function psychologically. This may involve addictions, habitual behaviours, or the social roles they are required to perform. Repetition may be a factor, as people become tired or disgusted with doing, feeling and thinking the same way day after day. Ultimately, due to understimulation, people can become plain bored with themselves and their lives.

Whether the confrontation is with the external circumstances of their life or internally with themselves, the end result is the same: they reach a turning point, a key moment of decision, in which they are confronted with their own inadequacies and pains.

Turning points are crucial moments in individuals' lives because they involve new non-habitual feelings and thoughts. These feelings and thoughts infuse an individual with fresh energy. This energy is sufficient to interrupt or even radically change a life's momentum. But the energy can also be frittered away.

Frittering away new energy most commonly occurs when people join a special interest group, whether a church, a political party, or a club of hobbyists, and channel their dissatisfaction into a social activity that ends up distracting them from the pain generated by their confrontation with their self. The opportunity to change is then diverted into self-calming. Psychologically, instead of confronting themselves they distract themselves. As a result, the new energy drains away.

On the other hand, radical change may result when individuals use the new energy to look into themselves, to examine their routines, roles and behaviours, and to review what they wish to achieve during the remainder of their life. At such times, impulses emanating from the spiritual self have a chance resonate within individuals' everyday awareness. The result is that individuals may be reminded of their life plan and life goal.

Such turning points occur rarely in a life, perhaps only once. But they are crucial if individuals are to break out of the constrictions generated by biological urges and social conditioning. They are crucial if you wish to take charge of your life.

These moments of self-review, these turning points, have various names. Mid-life crisis has become a fashionable term. In the past, given that humanity's social environment was governed by religion, people thought of these moments as crises of faith. The result was that people began doubting their religion, or they had a conversion experience and threw themselves anew into their religion. But, of course, at heart the crisis was not of faith in their religion or God, the crisis was with respect to their unhappiness with themselves and the life they were living.

The Greeks called the outcome of such moments *metanoein*, in English metanoia. This literally refers to changing your mind, changing your way of thinking. For this change to have lasting impact, you need to review those aspects that are most precious in your life, such as world view, values, morality, and your ideas regarding who, what and why you are who you are. Because personal identity is so bound up in these things, self-confrontation is perhaps the most difficult of all human activities. But it is necessary in order to achieve real, lasting inner change.

In the next book in this series, *Psychological Spirituality*, we will examine in detail how to crack and change the crystallised self and so alter a life's momentum. For now we return the discussion to the wider context of how a spirit uses embodiment to achieve its life goals.

PART TWO

REINCARNATION AND THIS LIFE

CHAPTER 8

What is the Purpose of a Life?

THESE ARE THE AGE-OLD QUESTIONS that have haunted human beings across the millennia: Who am I? What am I made of? What is soul and spirit? What is God? Why has the world come into existence? Is there a reason life occurs and I am here? What should I be doing with the opportunity? What is the best way to act and to live?

It is possible to answer these questions in high-faluting terms, using profound concepts and quoting impressive authorities and sacred texts. But it is not necessary to do so. At the risk of being deflationary, the purpose of a life is simple and straight forward. A spirit's incarnation in a body gives it the opportunity to experience the complexities of human existence, and in doing so to grow as a spiritual identity. Being human is nothing more, or less, than this.

Spiritual identities incarnate in a physical body on countless planets throughout the universe and in all kinds of different physical forms. So the occurrence of embodiment is far from rare. Indeed, it is exceedingly common. However, for individual spiritual identities intimately involved in the experiences of their personal existence, each incarnation as a human being is a momentous and significant event. Why? Because the process involves them personally in their evolution as a fragment of spiritual consciousness.

Evolution occurs in increments. Each incarnation provides an opportunity for spiritual identities to progress their development. While human beings find this difficult to accept, many of the most significant experiences they undergo during the course of each lifetime are pre-planned. Key conflicts, significant relationships, primary and ongoing difficulties (whether with oneself or with others), and struggles to succeed at a particular occupation, task or line of activity are all pre-planned before a life is begun. Of course, chance can throw a randomising element into the mix, presenting unplanned problems and opportunities that may end up dominating an entire life. Nonetheless, to speak generally, the most challenging situations, which if addressed and resolved successfully lead to the most satisfying outcomes, are selected and organised before the spiritual identity incarnates.

This spiritual fact puts into context the different aspects of the five-layered self that we have just been discussing. Essence traits are deliberately chosen pre-life on the basis that they provide useful moving, emotional and intellectual attributes. Drawing on and growing these attributes provides human beings with their primary essence level goals, goals that are selected in order to promote the spirit's ongoing evolution.

Similarly, a particular body is selected because it provides a set of specific genetically defined predispositions. The cultural environment the body is born into provides physical and social conditions that are also chosen to facilitate inner growth. In particular, the social environment, including the five factors discussed in the previous chapter, in some ways help the individual achieve essence goals and in some ways impede their realisation. Drawing on positive and nurturing factors, and struggling against negative and hindering factors, helps individuals in their overiding task of evolving as spiritual identities. For this reason hindering factors are as important as nurturing factors. In each life there needs to be a balance of each.

NURTURING AND HINDERING FACTORS

Nurturing factors encourage an individual to pursue a line of development, while hindering factors provide circumstances and adversaries to fight, struggle against and climb over. Fighting, struggling and climbing over develop and embed positive qualities in each person's psychospiritual make-up, qualities that help them become stronger, more knowledgeable and more capable.

This same pattern of pre-selection, nurturing, hindering, struggling and overcoming is repeated over the course of every lifetime. In each life essence level abilities are consolidated, and negative and limiting essence traits grow or diminish, depending on how much effort the individual puts into feeding, fighting, suppressing or transforming them.

Accordingly, just as biological, social and essence factors are deliberately chosen pre-birth, during each life individuals also have a choice with respect to how they deal with what they have chosen. The fact is that many people fight against their own choices, refusing to take up, or even destroying, opportunities they themselves created pre-life. As a consequence, they negate the hard work they did in previous incarnations to generate all the positive possibilities they organised for themselves to pursue in this current life.

None of this hard work is lost, of course. But it does mean that sometimes lives are much more difficult than was planned, because individuals torpedo their own self-chosen and pre-organised opportunities. What wakes people up to self-selected opportunities are inner cues.

INNER CUES

Inner cues come from the spiritual self. They consist of inner impulses that manifest in the everyday awareness as feelings, thoughts or as an inexplicable urge to make a certain choice or to follow a particular line of activity.

This is where dealing intelligently with the limiting aspects of daily physical and socialised existence is important. When individuals wholly surrender to the push and pull of everyday existence, allowing themselves to be driven by bodily urges, social agendas and social identity, they may certainly have a lifetime of fascinating experiences. But immersion in conditioned human interactions also causes them to miss the many inner cues that come into their everyday awareness. And by missing those inner cues they miss utilising the opportunities they themselves chose before they were born.

Becoming spiritual involves establishing an inner state whereby one learns to recognise those cues, then works out how best to act on them. At first such cues are hazy, half-perceived, half guessed at. Initially the individual is left wondering whether the cue is real or imagined. But over time, if the individual pays attention to the subtle cues that occasionally enter everyday awareness, the haze gradually clears and the cues start being perceived for what they are.

This is where the spiritual self plays a far more significant role in making key life choices than is generally understood. It is the spiritual identity who, pre-life, selects the essence self's genetic disposition and traits, chooses the body and its attendant physical, social and cultural environment, and decides on primary roles, habitual behaviours and possibly even key conditioned reactions. It selects them to provide optimal conditions for its learning and progress in its forthcoming incarnation.

In addition, the spiritual identity also chooses key life tasks and goals for the purpose of learning and evolving. When opportunities arise to use essence traits, and to realise key tasks and goals, it is the spiritual self that provides the cues that subtly manifest in the individual's everyday awareness. These cues enable the individual, on the embodied physical level, to recognise the opportunity that has arrived. The spiritual self then urges the individual to act on its cue and to pursue what is on offer. This is an example of the spiritual self entering the domain of the everyday and guiding its human sub-identity.

Unfortunately, giving, perceiving and responding to cues is not always as straight forward as this suggests. If an individual's everyday awareness is dominated by the crystallised socialised self, and that self is full of assumptions and fears projected onto it via cultural conditioning, then the individual is highly likely to ignore the cue. Indeed, because it is caught up in biological and social activities, the individual may not even be aware that a cue has arrived. In this way people ignore opportunities to advance their own psychospiritual development, opportunities they themselves generated.

However, in the context of the ongoing growth of any spiritual identity, it needs to be made clear that this is not a bad thing. There is no stigma attached to declining to respond to an inner cue. It is nothing more, or less, than a wasted opportunity. Other opportunities will be organised to be fulfilled in future incarnations. Nonetheless, given that the purpose of human existence is to learn, grow and evolve, consistently turning away from pre-planned opportunities (and some individuals certainly do this) leads to an unnecessarily long dalliance in the human domain. In the wider context of overall spiritual evolution, this is fine. But it remains a shame, given the vast number of post-human opportunities that yet await in the universe. And beyond.

Being incarnated is all about recognising opportunities and acting on them. Those opportunities are yours. You chose them pre-birth. They exist for you to do with as you please. You can ignore them. You can do the bare minimum with them. Or you can pick them up and use them as wings to fly. Your life, with all its attendant pleasures, hassles, pains, boredom, stress, love, fullness and emptiness, is yours. Do with it as you will!

Having clarified this, we next need to consider in greater detail how precisely reincarnation impacts on life opportunities and choices.

CHAPTER 9

Reincarnation and Deep Essence

THAT REINCARNATION IS A CRUCIAL FACTOR in human spiritual becoming is a concept that is increasingly familiar to people worldwide. However, the Western world view remains powerfully influenced by Christianity and scientific atheism, both of which, despite their fundamental differences, agree that human beings have only one shot at living a life.

Nonetheless, and perhaps as a result of exposure to Eastern religious teachings, the concept of reincarnation is today increasingly being explored as people grapple with the nature of their existence. Yet misconceptions about reincarnation cloud its proper appreciation. This includes ideas such as that human beings may reincarnate as animals and the idea that reincarnation is linked to status and caste. Neither is the case.

As was stated in the introduction, in this book reincarnation is assumed as a fact of human existence. No arguments will be offered in support of this contention. Those who doubt human reincarnation will need to do their own research in order to confirm or deny its occurrence. Research is required because falling back on conditioning or prejudice to deny (or accept) the idea of reincarnation, without exploring the growing body of material related to reincarnation that is currently available, and without considering the concept in relation to life experiences, is merely to decide arbitrarily and in ignorance.

Of course, many people *need* to reject the concept of reincarnation, because accepting it would wreck havoc on their religiously or scientifically shaped worldviews. The defensive behaviours of denying, justifying, deflecting and attacking are as commonly used in relation to the concept of reincarnation as with any other potentially life-changing idea.

For all who lack confirming evidence regarding reincarnation, and who understandably are therefore undecided, a request is made that you read the following with an open mind and that you weigh what is stated against key events from your own life. For, ultimately, it is only in the context of your own life experiences that the validity of reincarnation may be tested and verified.

WHY REINCARNATE?

The reason for reincarnation is straightforward. Individuals cannot undergo all the experiences that are part of being human, cannot learn all there is to learn from the experience of being human, in just one lifetime. Given the richness of human culture, the manifold and complex ways that human beings interact, and all the innumerable possibilities for human experience and achievement, one lifetime is not sufficient to explore the full bounty of experiences that being human gives access to.

Imagine playing one game of football, and from that single experience expecting to become an expert player. Clearly, this is an unrealistic expectation. No matter how much natural talent one may possess, becoming an expert footballer is a growth process that requires tremendous focus, commitment and hard work. The same applies to becoming an experienced, knowing and understanding human being.

Over the course of multiple incarnations each individual gets to experience the full emporium of human delights and horrors. Each incarnates as man and woman, and in between. Each tries out different occupations, explores all the permutations of human relationships, and develops many kinds of expertise. Each experiences dying young, dying old, achieving goals and failing to achieve goals. Each experiences bliss and deep unhappiness.

Of course, it is not necessary to try absolutely every human experience. You will likely be killed at some time during the course of your incarnations. But you do not have to kill. As a spiritual core consciousness you can choose how you wish to live in a human body. You may choose to learn to make art but not to play a musical instrument. You may prefer one centre over the other two and so concentrate on developing that centre's prowess. You may spend lives developing one particular kind of expertise. It is entirely up to you what you do with the opportunities provided by repeated human incarnation.

But behind all the choices is one aim: to experience life as a human being and to use those experiences to learn and to grow. Learning and growth in turn lead to the acquisition of the knowledge and understanding that contributes to the expansion of each person's core spiritual consciousness.

The key to learning and growing is accumulation. What is learnt during the course of each life, what is developed through personal effort, what is accomplished as a result of overcoming obstacles, all this accumulates within and is carried from one incarnation into those that follow. Self-limiting and negative psychological traits that are not overcome are also accumulated and carried into subsequent lives.

This means that no one has been born into this life as a blank slate. You have brought much with you. Some factors and traits facilitate growth. Some hinder it. Achievements do not vanish. And neither do obstacles. Reaping what you have sown, exploring what confronts you, and facing up to the consequences of what you do, feel and think, life by life, is all part of the process of accumulating experience, knowledge and understanding and growing spiritually. These next seven chapters explore the impact past lives have on any individual's current life journey. We'll begin with a consideration of deep essence.

DEEP ESSENCE AND THE ESSENCE SELF

As was stated earlier, during the course of each incarnation a spiritual identity selects, and experiences human life via, a sub-identity. This sub-identity is born with certain traits, which it develops, or does not, in accordance with its desires. When that sub-identity dies the experiential data generated during the course of that life is uploaded to the ongoing spiritual identity.

The data accumulated from all such human sub-identities may be called deep essence. Deep essence is the accumulation of all the essence level moving, emotional and intellectual qualities and traits that the spiritual identity has experienced, manifested and explored through its many sub-identities.

It must be made clear that deep essence refers to human level qualities, not to spiritual level qualities. Although, the two are linked. For example, a spiritual core consciousness can only express love within the human domain to the extent that the individual's essence level development facilitates it. The spiritual identity is all love. But it can only manifest that love in the human domain via its essence self. So the essence self has to be "tuned" into loving. This requires overcoming all the limiting psychological traits that prevent the individual from being perfectly loving. To achieve this individuals need to conquer the pettiness inherent in human social interactions, along with their own biases and defensiveness, as these all inhibit the full expression of love.

A moment's reflection on what has happened during your life, especially reflecting on the choices and reactions you made that you subsequently wished you had not, that you later even came to deeply regret, indicates that being perfectly loving is not natural to human existence. It has to be learned. And not in one lifetime, but over a considerable number of lives.

The same principle applies to any essence level activity. It has its roots in the spiritual identity. But because the spiritual identity necessarily expresses itself via the human essence self, that expression is never instantly and naturally the fullest it can be. Mastery has to be acquired. And mastery is only ever acquired over the course of multiple lifetimes.

While those lifetimes are being lived, each sub-identity develops both positive and negative traits. Over repeated incarnations, as the ongoing spiritual identity works towards mastery in the experience of being incarnated, the percentage of negative to positive traits gradually declines. But this means that, from one life to another, negative qualities linger among the positive. When a life comes to an end, and that particular sub-identity expires, those negative qualities are uploaded to the spiritual self and so become part of its trove of deep essence qualities.

When it subsequently comes time for the spiritual identity to decide what it will select for its next incarnation, it chooses from among both the positive and negative qualities present in its deep essence. In order to gain mastery in any area of human endeavour, whether that involves being perfectly loving, or perfectly musical, or a perfect viticulturalist, perfect architect, perfect builder or perfect parent, there are certain qualities that in previous lives have enhanced the spirit's full positive expression in that domain and other qualities that have hindered the spirit's full positive expression. The spirit chooses some (but usually not all) of the limiting and negative qualities, along with some previously engendered positive qualities, so that the next incarnation may best be used as an opportunity to explore a particular facet of human existence and to overcome the negativities associated with that facet.

Thus when the spirit selects and enters a new body, it brings with it certain pre-chosen essence qualities that become embedded in its new essence self. In this way each current essence self contains and reflects past accomplishments and failures. This explains how a child may be musical or artistic, or have green fingers, or be a natural cook or teacher, when no one in the family displays these abilities. Even if a child is both naturally musical and born into a musical family (so the gene pool and family conditioning naturally reinforce an innate music ability), the *way* that the child is musical, the particular qualities that she or he brings to music making, will reflect deep essence qualities.

No sub-identity is an island. It stands in its local social environment, it has caves filled with genetically inherited essence qualities, and those caves are linked by very deep subterranean tunnels that connect it to past lives.

ESSENCE IS CHOSEN

From this it can seen that the qualities present in an individual's essence are never present arbitrarily. If someone is naturally mechanical, or a computer geek, or a nurse, or artistic, or mothering, or a lover of extreme sports, that particular essence quality is no accident. Even if individuals feel that they accidentally fell into their profession, to the extent that that profession accords with the qualities and drives of their essence self, no accident is involved.

Similarly, life tasks and life goals always reflect essence qualities and involve essence level fulfilment. Even when opportunities existing in the social environment are clearly and necessarily involved in fulfilling life tasks and goals, it is at the essence level that the real play is occurring, not at the social level – with the ultimate aim throughout being that the situation offers the spiritual identity a further opportunity to develop personal mastery.

Two other factors impact significantly on the way the spiritual self uses the essence self to explore human experience. These are karma and life goal.

CHAPTER 10

The Impact of Karma

WE HAVE JUST CONSIDERED THE EXTENT to which an individual's life is psychologically impacted by character traits developed in previous lives. Prior to birth individuals draw on those traits to shape the psychology of their next sub-identity. Past experiences, particularly experiences which in some sense were left incomplete or unresolved, also impact on what individuals do in their next life. What an individual does, or at least sets out to do, during the course of a life is embodied in the life plan and its related life goals. These are devised before incarnating. A significant factor that feeds into the life plan and its goals is what has become known as karma.

Karma has been viewed differently by different cultures, but it has usually been linked to retribution. That is, karma is conceived as involving re-paying for misdemeanours or worse done in this or prior lives. The concept of karma as retribution leads people to reason that someone who tortures, rapes or enslaves another individual in one life will in turn be tortured, raped or enslaved in their next life – that they will have to pay for bad deeds carried in this life by suffering through the same actions in the next. The flipside of this reasoning is that someone who is tortured, raped or enslaved in this life must deserve it because they were bad in a previous life. Such thinking has given rise to the contemporary concept that people accumulate bad karma that will need to be paid for at some time in the future.

All this reasoning is overly-simplistic, if not outright wrong. No karma is bad. Or good. Karma is simply another aspect of human existence that needs to be faced up to and worked through.

THE IMPACT OF KARMA

In Sanskrit, *karma* means action. Today karma is usually taken to refer to consequence, hence the idea that some karma is good and some is bad. In contradistinction to this common view, the word karma is being used here to refer to an action, that action's motivation, and the consequence: karma = motivation + action + consequence. They form a unit of karma, so to speak. Hence when considering the consequences of an action, what motivated the action in the first place needs to be considered. Of course, such consideration is relatively easy when action and consequence are separated by only minutes, hours or days. But understanding the link between a consequence in this life and its causative action in a previous life is far more difficult.

To return to the concept of supposed bad karma, naturally some actions have negative consequences for the perpetrator and those impacted by the action. Other actions have positive consequences. But the karma is not bad or good in itself. Because, in fact, all actions and consequences lead to human experience, and all experiences, once fully processed and digested, lead to growth. Naturally, in retrospect some actions come to be viewed as helpful and some as unhelpful, some as constructive and some as destructive. Yet all equally offer opportunities to learn and grow. In fact, as the homily says, you often learn more from your mistakes than you do from what you get right.

So while a portion of karma certainly does involve making mistakes and making up for or repaying for those mistakes, in fact the reasons people make mistakes in the first place are often very complex. Few mistakes arise from individuals being outright "bad" in any sense. Errors of judgement, over-enthusiasm, over-commitment, spontaneous reaction, weaknesses and quirks of character, self-defensiveness, poor or biased perception, even a desire to do the right thing, can lead to unintended, catastrophic consequences. As the daily news also makes clear, an action or set of actions may simultaneously generate beneficial consequences for some and limiting consequences for others – and we are talking psychologically as well as materially.

What this means is that while a portion of karma is certainly focused on correcting past errors and mistakes, the ways that karma contributes to the shaping of a life actually has much more to do with generating experiences by which an individual can re-address a situation experienced in a previous life and attempt to do it better next time round.

The goal is to do it right, given that doing it right consists of making choices and applying them in a knowing and loving way that takes into account everyone involved. It takes multiple lifetimes to learn how to deal with complex situations and transform poor performance first into better performance, then into doing it right and benefiting rather than impinging on others.

APPRECIATING THE IMPACT OF KARMA

From what we have just stated, it is clear that coming to appreciate how karma accrued in a previous life is playing out in this life is not easy. As noted, getting to grips with the depths of human psychology is a complex and demanding task. It is even more difficult to understand how karma weaves across a sequence of lives, threading through repeated situations, choices and outcomes, and contributing to the drama not just of your life but to others' lives, all of whom have their own different emphases and perspectives.

Glib judgements that someone is getting what they deserve, or that high or low status in this life indicates a person having been good or bad in a prior life, or for individuals to put themselves down because their life is not as successful, significant, colourful or as rich as someone else's, are not just superficial; deeper insight will reveal them to be plain wrong.

To appreciate how karma impacts on your life involves considerable introspection. You need to consider a situation from multiple perspectives. Why? Because significant events in any life are very rarely structured via simple cause and effect.

First, there is the matter of your own psychological make-up that has contributed to the generation of the situation. Certain traits will have led you to make the choices you have. If you ran away or were confrontational, you need to understand exactly *how* you ran away or were confrontational?

Second, other people are invariably involved in your choices. So their psychological make-up also needs to be taken into account, particularly those traits that led them first to become involved in your situation, and then caused them to react in the ways they did.

Third, there is the relationship between you and these other people. At what level are you attached? On which of the biological, social, essence, energetic or spiritual levels? Very likely you are attached on more than one. All this needs to be understood.

Fourth, there is the question as to what in your past lives is feeding the current situation. Are you working out or resolving the consequences of some prior choice or commitment you made? If so, what exactly? The playing out of consequences functions on both positive and negative lines. For example, in an earlier incarnation you may have decided to develop your potential in a certain area of human endeavour. So in this life you are continuing to live out that self-commitment. This is all positive. Alternatively, you may previously have committed errors that you are now working to correct. Naturally, in working through the consequences of prior life errors you currently have no conscious recollection of when, where, why or how you did what you did. You may feel grief, or shame, or be depressed, without knowing why. Now you just feel driven, at the level of your everyday awareness, and despite your ignorance of the prior life deeper factors, to do what you are doing. Intense digging is required in order to understand how everything you are experiencing and going through is linked to other lives.

Fifth, others who are involved in your commitment to work through karma have their own reasons for being with you. They may have vowed to work positively with you, so you are both striving towards the same goal. Or they may have taken on the role of antagonist, providing you with an obstacle to overcome. Hence at the socialised level an antagonist may be undermining your endeavours, yet at the spiritual level they are as committed as you are, helping you achieve your goal. Thus an antagonist fulfils the very useful role of generating experiences that aid your deep level growth.

All these factors need to be considered when you attempt to understand the way karma contributes to your life journey this time round. To provide an image, if you imagine a single situation as a point in space and time, numerous threads, some possibly coming from thousands of years and many lives away, have been drawn together to form the knot that is that one situation. This is why human drama is so complex – and is so difficult to untangle. The fact is that human life has many levels, and multiple contributing factors at each level, that generate tangles of motivation, behaviour, choices and consequences.

On the other hand, once you identify a thread, and you track back where it leads, that introspective activity will gradually illuminate other threads that feed into the knot. And, by degrees, the knot will start untangling. Of course, this takes sustained effort. But the reward is that you will begin to understand how what you are and do now has been shaped by choices you previously made.

To help begin this process of unravelling the knot we'll look at the idea of karma as involving impinging on others.

IMPINGING GENERATES KARMA

During the course of living with groups of people, individuals inevitably impinge on each others. Sometimes impinging occurs with strangers. But by far the majority of impinging occurs among those who come into frequent contact with each other due to living, working or playing together.

Much impinging is minor, such as when people rub others the wrong way, whether with habits, words or attitudes, leading to small arguments or spats that flare briefly then die away. No significant karma accrues from these types of interactions. However, repeated negative interactions may need to be worked through in a later incarnation and put to bed, so to speak. More important is when individuals maintain habits, or project attitudes or biases, that repeatedly grate with others, causing them to react negatively or even to shy away. This involves minor karma. The individual manifesting such behaviour clearly needs to examine their psychology and address their impinging behaviours.

Other impinging is at what can be termed the intermediate level. This type of impinging affects others much more significantly and detrimentally. It includes suppressing and oppressing others to such a degree that they sustain a significant psychological wound, a wound that prevents them from achieving what they set out to do during this particular life.

Parents, of course, frequently do this. But parental-child relationships are usually factored into a life plan prior to incarnation. So, for example, an overbearing father or a undermining mother (or visa versa) may psychologically wound their child, but usually this wounding has already been designed as an obstacle the spirit incarnated in the child has decided to use to work with this time round. Where this intermediate level impinging usually occurs is outside immediate family relationships. It applies to situations that were not pre-planned, such as when a relative or priest molests a child, or when a worker takes a disliking to a co-worker and decides to sabotage the progress of their career.

This is a case where making broad-stroke generalisations becomes difficult, because child molestation may be planned prior to incarnation and involve a complex working through of historical inter-relationships. Appreciating whether a particular act of impinging is planned or not planned is crucial to understanding whether karma is being accumulated or being worked through.

By way of an example, let's say child molestation takes place that was not pre-planned. This means that one individual has decided to impinge on another – and being driven by urges they cannot control is still a chosen activity, because that balance of urge and lack of control is selected and acted on. As a result karma accrues between the individuals involved. How so?

Let's look at the child who is molested by an adult trusted by the family. A current example of this type of molestation, recently much in the news, is of a priest visiting a couple's home and molesting one of their children. If being molested wasn't in the life plan of that child, and a psychological trauma results that destabilises the child to such a degree that in later years he or she is unable to engage in activities or form relationships with particular people that were planned prior to incarnation, then the impinging individual has generated an intermediate level karmic link with the molested individual. This karmic link needs to be addressed. Because impinging individuals are rarely able to own up to and resolve what they have done during the course of the life in which they impinged, they will have to work through the consequences of their impinging in a later incarnation. Hence an agreement will need to be made between the two individuals directly involved to meet again in another life and resolve what exists between them.

In this case, because one individual has interrupted the potential life of the other, a redressing is required in which the perpetrator repays the victim. However, in describing this repaying we hesitate here to use the words "sin", "guilt", "reparation", even "make up for", or any other judgementally loaded words. Subtle thinking needs to be applied when considering the relationship that results when two people come together to work through karmic relationships. Superficially, in the case of molestation, it may appear that the karmic link is necessarily one-sided. After all, one individual damaged the other ruining that individual's life.

Yet each and every incarnation offers a range of experiences. Sometimes experiences are undergone that were unsought. But unsought experiences are experiences nonetheless, and so need to be processed exactly the same as pre-planned and sought experiences. So to step back and take a wide perspective, we would change the usual terminology of "perpetrator" into "facilitator of experience", and the terminology of "victim" into "surprised experiencer". This is not to excuse perpetrators' physical and psychological damage to others or to make light of what they do. It is rather an attempt to place a single event, that happened in one particular lifetime, into the context of multiple events that occur over hundreds of lifetimes. In this wider context, each and every experience, whether planned or unplanned, sought or unsought, anticipated or surprising, welcomed or spurned, enjoyed or hated, becomes no more or less than another opportunity to learn and grow. This applies to everyone who is involved.

In the case of molestation, the initiator needs to use the experience to learn how to control his/her bodies' sexual urges, along with the psychological traits that lead him/her to impinge on a child who was not able to fight back, as opposed to an adult who would be more able to do so. And the surprised experiencer has an opportunity to learn to deal with the trauma of the physical event, along with the negative psychological impacts that occur at the level of the biological and socialised selves, but that likely also impact on and distort the essence level emotions. We repeat, this is not to excuse the molester. It is merely to point out that all experiences, once they have occurred, need to be processed, deep understanding extracted from them, and the inward consequences worked through and resolved. Finally, even after each individual involved has dealt with their own psychological motivations and reactions to the incident, a personal link remains between the two. This link needs to be addressed so it loses its quality of negative binding.

The usual psychological working through in relation to traumatic events applies in this situation, such as being able to forgive, dealing with rage or resentment or a sense of failure or of guilt. Ultimately, each needs to lose all sense of being either a victimiser or a victim. Attachment to being a victim is as large an issue as victimising others, indeed they can be linked, with childhood victims becoming adult victimisers. Basically, all resentments, negative attitudes, and self-limiting projections and reactions need to be dissolved so that the relationship between the two individuals concerned becomes warm and loving with no sense of anything left unsaid or undone. This, of course, is on the spiritual level. But because the karmic link has been generated at the level of human incarnation, it must be dissolved on the human level. Clearly, this is a demanding outcome, especially if the "facilitator of experience" has behaved like a monster. Nonetheless, all negative links must be transformed into positive links.

Major impinging occurs when an individual kills another, or maims them to such a degree that they are unable to carry out their chosen life tasks. The difference between intermediate and major impinging is a matter of degree. For example, if a priest molested a child once, and as a result caused psychological trauma that negatively impacted on only some aspects of the child's subsequent life, that would be intermediate level impinging. But if the molestation was sustained and involved rape and physical and psychological damage, such as has been the case when fathers lock up their daughters in the basement and treat them as sex slaves for years, then that is likely to result in major karma.

Why do we say only "likely"? Because in all this there is still the response of the surprised experiencer to take into account. If she is psychologically resilient the experience may not derail the rest of her life. In that case the father may be a monster (at least in this sub-identity), yet despite his monstrous behaviour major karma has not been accrued. Nonetheless, a karmic link has certainly been formed that will need to be worked through.

Hence to differentiate between intermediate and major karma is useful for the sake of discussion, yet in practice such labels can be arbitrary, and even inhibit full understanding of what occurred. Anyone seeking to understand levels of karmic impinging also need to ensure they keep judgement out of their thinking. We repeat, subtle thinking is required in order to understand the ways that karma impacts on a life.

QUESTIONS OF KARMIC CONSEQUENCES

One question that naturally arises in discussions of karma is what of those politicians and generals who order the killing of others? They are not actually dropping the bomb or pulling the trigger, so do they accrue karma in relation to the killings? And what about those who just follow orders, yet are directly responsible for causing the deaths of others and so preventing those individuals from fulfilling their life goals? What karmic links are generated by them?

Killing anonymously, so to speak, under orders, does not generate either major or intermediate karma. No direct relationships are formed between those who follow orders to bomb or shoot and those who are killed. However, if those in, say, a helicopter take it into their own hands to arbitrarily shoot up a group on the ground, no matter whether they are motivated by blood lust, boredom, bravado, or by any other trait, a karmic link is formed between shooters and shot that will have to be worked through.

With respect to politicians, leaders or criminals who are publicly viewed as monsters because their choices led to the deaths of many, the key question to appreciating the karmic links they accrue is discovering what drives them. Some enjoy killing, to the extent that they are present at deaths. They may even carry out killings themselves. In doing so they accrue major karmic links with all those they kill or cause to be killed.

But for others the situation may be that they have reached a position of power and the position gets away on them. They may have decided, pre-life, that this time round they want to try being a ruler. But once they are in the position they discover that they are not as psychologically resilient as they thought, and are certainly not strong enough to handle the pressures involved. They may then end up relying on others who manipulate the situation to their own ends. Or their everyday awareness may become so overwhelmed by the number and complexity of the inputs involved in leading that they lose their psychological and moral bearings and order things to happen that, in their unstressed state, they certainly would not have. They may also need to make decisions and be incapable of processing the consequences of those decisions.

Positions of leadership generate their own momentum. Some individuals are able to steer that momentum. Others ride it successfully, for a short or long time, then jump off. Others lose their balance, fall, and get smashed by it. For all these individuals a significant consequence of their experience is that they need to appreciate why they wanted to be in such a role when they were unable to handle it. They also have to address the fact that they impinged on others during the course of losing control. And they need to address the consequences of losing control in a way that is appropriate and gets to the essence of what motivated them and that generated whatever consequently occurred.

Our intention in discussing karma in these terms is to indicate that while there are degrees of impinging, and so degrees of karmic links that are generated, to really appreciate for yourself the way that karma impacts on your life, you need to view karma in the light of your own relationships. Because, essentially, it is in relationships that karma plays out, whether those relationships involve accruing or working out and resolving karmic links.

AGREEMENTS

In order for a karmic link to be resolved, the individuals involved need to be reincarnated in proximity to each other. If they never come into contact, clearly karma cannot be resolved. This means that prior to incarnating individuals need to make an agreement to meet and work through whatever exists between them. Essentially, individuals make agreements prior to incarnation to meet during their life journeys in order to facilitate learning and growth. As we have already noted, sometimes the agreement is for one to take on the role of antagonist and push the other. At other times individuals decide to work alongside each other.

In addition, agreements may be for long or short durations. Prior to incarnating two individuals may agree to sustain a relationship over a whole lifetime, likely by living or working together. These extended connections may involve close or distant relationships, depending on what each requires and agrees to. In some lives an agreement is made to meet only a handful of times, or even just once. The purpose of such brief meetings may be that one arrives in another's life at a crucial moment and helps give her or him a push in a desired direction. Or it may be as simple as involving a mutual affirmation, then moving on.

In many lives an agreement may be made to "hang out". No deep experiencing or learning is involved. It is simply a matter of old friends, at the spiritual level, spending time together during the course of an incarnation. Again this may be for a short or long period. Why do so? Because incarnation can be trying. And having long-term spiritual friends around, whether as support or to comfort, helps make the life journey easier and trying times less of a struggle.

All this leads to the idea of soul mate. Much has been written in spiritual and psychological literature about the virtues of finding your soul mate in this life. Many people have the view that finding your soul mate is in fact necessary to living a successful and satisfying life. In general, this literature over romanticises the relationship between individual spirits.

Certainly soul mates exist. But no one has just one. During the course of repeated incarnations everyone develops relationships with a number of fellow travellers with whom they live, laugh, fight, work and play. Each of these soul friends have their particular strengths and weaknesses, abilities and talents. Naturally, individuals consider what each of their soul friends has to offer when planning their next life, and form agreements with one or more based on what each incarnating individual wants to achieve, taking into account whatever skills and expertise their soul friends may bring to the table. On the other hand, sometimes two individuals just decide to get together during incarnation and see what they might get up to, without any great plan, just to enjoy hanging out. All this is possible.

The upshot is that you have no single soul mate who is the one and only individual who completes you. Rather, you have a group of friends at the spiritual level who you get together with in some lives and not in others. These friends facilitate opportunities, spur each other on, and help one another during their struggles to learn and grow. The number of these friends depends entirely on the individuals concerned. Some individuals are garrulous at the spiritual level, being loving and giving, and so form extensive and deep friendship. Others are more introverted, reticent even. Some like to experiment and enter a life with few friends around, in order to meet new individuals and to test how they cope. Others prefer to keep a soul friend close at all times. All this occurs. It merely depends on innate disposition and choice.

RESOLVING KARMA

When considering the impact of karma on your life, the consequences of major life events are the most obvious and easily observed part of the karmic equation. They are what people can't help but observe. They are what everyone gets caught up in.

But, really, in terms of learning and growing, it is the action, and especially what motivated the action in the first place, that is the most significant aspect. Certainly all individuals involved need to work through the consequences of impinging actions, resolving whatever is negative and has led to injury. But if the motivation is not dealt with, then the impinging individual will carry out the same action again. Thus resolution of motivation is essential to breaking the karmic chain. This is why we are emphasising the need for everyone to examine themselves psychologically. Our examination will continue with a consideration of the essence level life goal.

CHAPTER 11

The Seven Life Goals

PSYCHOLOGICALLY, EVERY HUMAN BEING has a single defining essence level life goal. This life goal denotes a fundamental approach to living that the spiritual identity has adopted. It underpins everything the individual is striving to achieve during this life.

As was made clear in the previous two chapters, the individual spirit draws on a number of factors when deciding how it will live its next incarnation. These factors include positive and negative deep essence qualities developed during previous lives, essence traits innate to the next body's genetic disposition, karma that is to be worked through, and agreements to meet certain other incarnated spiritual identities in order to help achieve mutually agreed tasks. All these are part of an individual's life plan.

Life plans vary hugely. Sometimes a life plan is full and complex, encompassing many tasks and involving many other individuals. Sometimes a life plan is very simple, embracing few tasks, with the life treated as time out because previous lives were demanding, even overwhelming, and the spirit has decided it needs an entire life to catch its breath and process what it previously did. Sometimes the spirit decides to focus on one significant objective during its next life, and so pre-arranges just one major decision, with a limited set of consequences, to be worked through. Sometimes the life plan is not to have much of a plan at all, with the spirit choosing a body and a set of initial physical and social conditions to be born into, then throwing caution to the winds and seeing what happens. However, in by far the majority of cases a life plan is worked out pre-life, in lesser or greater detail. It also needs to be observed that often life plans do not work out at all as planned. Nonetheless, a life is lived, often a fruitful life, and the plan remains to be revived in a new form in a subsequent life.

We'll come back to the life plan presently. For now we'll continue this examination of the implications of reincarnation by looking more closely at an individual's life goal. There are seven in total.

THE SEVEN LIFE GOALS

The life goal is a psychological characteristic that functions at the essence level. We note that the life goal being discussed here is not the same as what is generally referred to as life goals.

Life goals are specific pragmatic physical and social goals individuals set themselves to achieve during the course of a week, a month, a year, or even a lifetime. Life goals include taking part in a competition, establishing a career, having a family, becoming wealthy, dedicating one's life to helping the underprivileged, becoming a country's president or prime minister, or not being like one's parents or siblings. Life goals may be large or small. But they are physically or socially defined, and they all involve a series of steps or tasks that need to be accomplished in order to achieve the chosen life goals may be achieved. We call these life tasks.

In contrast, the *life goal* doesn't involve a particular task or series of tasks. The life goal may be thought of as psychological glue that underpins all the various aims, tasks, agreements, karmic debts, and essence activities that the individual chooses to carry out during the course of a life. As such, the life goal is aligned to each individual's life plan. The life goal defines the individual's overall approach to a life. Drawing again on the Michael Teachings, we identify seven fundamental types of life goal. These seven are: growth, revaluation, dominance, submission, acceptance, rejection and maintaining equilibrium. [See FIGURE 11.1.]

Each of these seven life goals identifies what, in global terms, an individual seeks to achieve in a particular life. It identifies an individual's approach, that is, an individual's essence level psychological predisposition, when faced with choices and alternative possibilities during any life.

At first glance these goals may seem somewhat simplistic, arbitrary even. But they provide a very useful rule-of-thumb for quickly identifying what individuals are striving to achieve in their life. It also explains some otherwise inexplicable decisions that people make, decisions that superficially appear to be contrary to the individual's overall life direction. Let's look at each in an introductory level of detail.

GROWTH

Growth is the most common of all the seven life goals. It drives an individual to seek new experiences, meet new people, undertake new tasks, and explore new opportunities. As a goal it may be broad or shallow. That is, it may be focused on a very narrow band of human experience and possibility, or it may be expansive and embrace a great diversity of experiences. An example of the first is a concert pianist who focuses on playing the piano for an entire lifetime, but constantly seeks to grow his performance. An example of the

THE SEVEN LIFE GOALS

	(+)	(−)
SELF-TRANSFORMING		
GROWTH	Comprehension	Confusion
RE-EVALUATION	Simplification	Withdrawal
SELF-ACTUALISING		
DOMINANCE	Leadership	Dictatorship
SUBMISSION	Devotion	Subservience
SELF-FULFILLING		
ACCEPTANCE	Agape	Ingratiation
REJECTION	Discrimination	Prejudice
SELF-NEUTRALISING		
EQUILIBIRUM	Suspension	Inertia

FIGURE 11.1

latter is a person who roams from one workshop or course to another, always trying new approaches and techniques and meeting new people.

The latter person has been labelled a course junky or workshop hound. In fact, the apparent inability to focus on any specific area of experience or knowledge may be a deliberate ploy by the incarnated spirit who is striving to break out of social, religious or psychological shackles taken on during prior incarnations. This behaviour may also be affected by negative psychological traits. Hence fear of rejection or of being intimately exposed may cause an individual to flit from one thing to the next, never staying long in any one place, group or discipline. An inability to focus, whether having its source in childhood conditioning, chemical imbalances in the body, or being driven by negativities such as greed or inadequacy, may divert the inner urge to grow, manifesting in behaviours that actually sabotage growth. This leads to inner confusion, as opposed to the greater comprehension that is developed by, for example, the focused concert pianist.

Growth occurs primarily on two levels. The first is within the essence self, with respect to its moving, emotional and intellectual capacities. In the case of a concert pianist, growth is facilitated when he uses his intellect to analyse the composition's architecture and intent, uses his emotions to connect with the music's inner qualities, and physically performs with the required dexterity. Each time a finger strikes a key the resulting note contains a combination of emotion, intellect and physical expertise. By challenging himself to think and feel ever more intensely and deeply and to perform with greater facility, the pianist's essence level moving, emotional and intellectual capacities grow.

The second level is spiritual. Whatever growth occurs within the essence self directly feeds the spiritual self. Why? Because the spiritual self resides at the individual's core, experiencing via the essence self all that the individual experiences during the course of everyday living. At the end of the life what is experienced, processed, developed and learned is then uploaded to the ongoing spiritual identity. In this way growth becomes key to the evolution of any spiritual identity's consciousness. It is also why growth is such a common life goal: because spiritual identities incarnate specifically in order to evolve.

However, there are many factors that inhibit and become obstacles to growth. In practice, obstacles are a positive because coming up against an obstacle focuses the attention of striving individuals, requiring them to make an even greater effort in order to complete their chosen tasks. Many obstacles are external, being present in physical and social environments. But ultimately the greatest obstacles are provided by inner attitudes, negative emotions, and limiting assumptions and beliefs. Determined individuals can overcome any external obstacle. But if they lack inner focus and drive nothing is achieved. Thus, by providing obstacles, the other layers of the self, especially the biological and social layers, stimulate the life goal of growth.

To illustrate all that growth involves, a scholar with a goal of growth would naturally desire to extend what he knows. In contrast, an artistic artisan with a goal of growth would be inclined to experiment creatively with new materials, textures, colours. And a king with a goal of growth would seek new territories to command, and not necessarily physical territories. In each case the positive expression of growth builds on what was previously achieved, so the scholar gains expertise in a branch of knowledge, the artisan develops high level creative skills, and the king learns better how to command a particular aspect of human interchange.

Inevitably, during the course of living a life the drive to grow is diverted and impeded by negativities. So the artistic artisan may find his work is rejected or ignored, and as a result starts to doubt himself and so lose heart. If he becomes increasingly cynical about the art world, this attitude is likely to negatively impact on his art-making. The scholar may wish to explore new intellectual territories, but finds the academic institution in which she works has other priorities and so she is required either to shift her underlying interests so they fit the institutional focus, or she may even have to give them up altogether. Depending on how much inner certainty she has – which reflects how much she is centred in her essence self, or how much her self-identity is tethered to social constructs – this situation will likely become an obstacle that needs to be overcome, otherwise it will lead to negative emotions such as frustration, self-pity or rage. Much more of the scholar's time would then be spent on dealing with inner negativities generated by the situation and less on progressing her study.

This need to deal with negativities that impinge on inner growth, that divert growth's momentum, or that halt it altogether, results in the other six life goals. They exist to help an incarnated spirit deal with a range of different negativities that have stopped them progressing in prior lives and that now need to be addressed in order to keep developing in the human sphere.

REVALUATION

At any time within a life journey an individual may choose to pause and evaluate what has occurred. This is a natural part of learning and growing. Without reflection, experiences are not processed and lessons not learned. In the case of those who have adopted a life goal of revaluation, this process is carried out not once but over the course of an entire lifetime.

Revaluation requires pausing and reflecting. These are passive activities. That is, they do not rely on having new experiences and meeting new people. On the contrary, undergoing new experiences would interfere with the reflective process. Rather, the individual's focus is directed onto what has already occurred, what has already been experienced, what has already been felt, thought and done. And not just in this life, but in prior lives.

The question then arises, how does this revaluating of prior lives play out in this life if the individual concerned doesn't remember their past lives – and it is the rare individual who does. The answer is that the individual organises a life situation that reflects a prior life situation. This current situation embodies issues the individual had previously had difficulty with and that now need to be worked through.

This "embodying of issues" usually occurs with the help of spiritual friends who incarnate with the individual and perform specific roles that generate the required situation. Some of these friends will play supportive roles, with others performing challenging and obstacle roles. In general, only one major situation is dealt with in this way in a single life. This is because it can be very complex putting the required factors and actors into place.

What hinders revaluation is the individual's own psychological reactions. The reason an individual takes on the life goal of revaluation in the first place is because in a number of prior lives what has been planned hasn't been achieved. A pattern of self-defensiveness is responsible for this inability. Accordingly, that self-defensiveness needs to be faced up to, then broken down. Only the individual can do this. We will explore how to do so in the next book in this series. For now we can say that breaking down one's self-defensive attitudes and behaviours is extremely difficult. Self-honesty is required, along with a sustained will to examine oneself, not shying away from unpleasant observations, and not blaming or deflecting onto others.

The life goal of revaluation is not common. Some individuals are able to evaluate their experiences and assess personal performance during their life's journey. Most individuals prefer to do this between lives, after they have completed one life and are beginning to plan the next.

The art of revaluation is to take the complex messiness of experiences in the human domain and boil them down to their underlying drivers. If you remain caught up in negative reactions such as guilt, rejection or blame, then the messiness continues to rule your emotions and head space. Negative reactions need to be cast aside in order to drill down to underlying psychological causes. In this sense, revaluation is a process of simplification. Conversely, those who remain caught up in their self-defensive behaviours end up withdrawing from the opportunity their life plan presents them and so fail to achieve what they set out to.

DOMINANCE

The next two life goals, dominance and submission, are two aspects of the one process, which is to develop balance within one's psychological make-up.

All spirits incarnating in the human domain aim to learn mastery. Much in human existence exists to prevent mastery. Daily life offers many temptations and diversions, whether by generating and fanning fears or by putting seemingly insurmountable obstacles in the way. In order to develop mastery individuals need to learn how to overcome the obstacles existing in their physical and social environments. In short, they need to learn how to dominate them. Because other human beings are always present in one's physical and social environments, and necessarily form part of what has to be overcome, those individuals need to be dominated.

Every single incarnated spiritual identity goes through the process of learning to dominate. However, it is a tricky skill to learn, because inevitably negativities slip into its performance, in the form of biases and prejudices, superficial judgement, self-defensiveness, self-doubt, over-eagerness, either pushing too hard or not pushing hard enough, being unable to read others' reactions, not responding adequately or quickly enough to others' reactions, and so on. The result is that performance of the life goal of dominance extends from sound leadership to oppressive dictatorship, with all the shades between.

Human beings are ambivalent about dominance. They applaud sportsmen and women who dominate others in their field of competition, admire businessmen and woman who make excessive amounts of money, and acknowledge scholars and writers whose work reveals new aspects of human existence and experience. But they fear politicians who gain excessive dominance over the populace, and they resent those who try to dominate their lives and control the circumstances of their daily existence, even if fear stops them doing anything in response.

Dominance is certainly a two-edged sword. Without striving for mastery of physical, emotional and intellectual skills, human existence would lack both richness and a deeper goal and purpose. But because it takes a number of lives to develop mastery, and negativities unavoidably seep into the process, those seeking to dominate their environment will inevitably be feared, resented or envied by some, while being applauded and encouraged by others.

The *Tao Te Ching* proposes that the sage leads from behind. That is, the sage acts as a rudder at the rear of the ship, guiding without being overt about it. Being able to do this involves mastery of human existence on a number of levels. To adapt other words of Lao Tzu, to be dominant without appearing to be dominant is to practise dominance with artistry.

SUBMISSION

As with dominance, so with submission. Every incarnating spirit has to learn to submit. People naturally think of dominance as reflecting strength while those who submit are weak. In fact, performed with mastery, both are manifestations of strength. And when poorly performed, each reflects weakness.

In the sense meant here, submission refers to becoming absorbed into an activity. This may involve joining a peace or environmental group, or a religious or academic school, or becoming a member of a sports team. In each case submission involves learning to play a role within that group. Doing so without becoming self-pitying or down-hearted because others are bigger, brighter, more naturally gifted, or more favoured requires true strength.

The performance of the life goal of submission extends from being devoted to one's cause, club, tribe or disciple, to being a subservient doormat. Subservience results when an individual goes into a situation as a result of negative impulses such as wanting to be accepted or loved, wanting others to appreciate one, or seeking to increase one's status or sense of self-worth.

These negative motivations must be separated from a neutral impulse such as lack. At some time in their lives everyone feels that they lack something they need. It could be a lack of knowledge, or of a skill set, even a lack of love. But the activity of filling that lack may be carried out in a positive or a negative way. For some, learning to dominate the situation they are in is the way forwards. For others learning to devote themselves to something they see as being greater or higher than themselves is required. But if either approach is pursued negatively, that is, if negative impulses infiltrate the process of filling the lack, then the process of learning submission is compromised.

In one sense, learning to dominate may be thought of as learning to lead, whereas learning to submit involves learning to be a follower. But the full performance of each requires a purification of one's layered self, the development of essence skills and positive psychological traits, and the acquisition of insights and understanding. With all these in place, the ultimate goal, which is to grow as a human being and to evolve as a spiritual identity, is much more fruitfully facilitated.

REJECTION

A second pair of life goals is rejection and acceptance. Where dominance and submission have to do with changing inner attitudes towards the world around one, rejection and acceptance have to do with how one interfaces with the world. There is a subtle difference involved here.

Submission and dominance manifest as inner drives within one's essence self that shape one's inner attitude towards the world – whether to strive to be devoted to an aspect of the human domain or to gain mastery over it. In contrast, rejection and acceptance involve the closing down or opening up of communication of one's self with the world. Rejection is a complex and difficult life goal. In any particular life rejection tends to be focused predominantly on either the outward or inward lines of communication. It may involve dealing with the rejection of external opportunities or alternatively with the rejection of inward capabilities, although in all cases rejection does involve a measure of both inward and outward rejection.

As with all the other life goals, rejection has both positive and negative applications. Its positive application is when incarnating spirits decide they have to learn to be more discriminating in the choices they make. During the course of every life each spirit develops certain psychological propensities, positive and negative, which enhance or inhibit inner growth. At the end of each life these propensities are uploaded to the ongoing spiritual self in the form of deep essence traits. Negative traits can build up over a number of lives, leading the incarnating spirit to decide to address a leading negative propensity or a number of lesser related traits.

To offer an example, a spirit which is developing its musical talent may be attracted to what was once a wandering or minstrel lifestyle, which manifests today as busking or gigging. This lifestyle offers opportunities for many indulgences, including excessive alcohol consumption, drug-taking, casual sex and general hard partying. An aspect of self-destructiveness is often also involved when the gigging lifestyle takes over from creative musicianship. If a spirit pursues this approach over a number of lifetimes, in the process self-limiting psychological propensities are generated that need to be disassembled. Such an individual may consequently choose the life goal of rejection in a subsequent series of lives in order to practise discrimination and thereby generate a more balanced inner psyche, so the everyday awareness is no longer as easily distracted by temptation or over-indulgence. This individual may live a number of comparatively dour and outwardly uneventful lives in order to develop strength of purpose. Naturally, the success of this strategy depends on the degree to which the individual addresses the particular negative deep essence attitudes and emotions that led him to choose the life goal of rejection in the first place.

The negative aspect of rejection is that the individual may become so caught up in rejection that the life's central lesson is missed. To continue the example of the musician, he may decide to begin life by being rejected by one or both parents. The purpose of organising this experience is to use the massive emotional shock to stimulate an approach to life in which he is naturally wary about engaging indiscriminately with others. In the context of his prior life debauchery, the purpose of this radical event is to encourage him to hold back. In effect, it is psychological shock treatment to help him stay sober.

But the risk with such a strategy is that self-indulgence has been a key underlying trait in his previous lives. And it is also present in this life, because it is one of the key traits he needs to address. So the risk is that the musician will get caught up in his feelings of parental rejection, then overcompensate and engage newly generated emotions such as distrust, uneasiness and aloofness. These are then likely to undermine his efforts to re-organise his psychological state into one in which he no longer indulges in his feelings. The problem is that instead of indulging in excessive partying as he did in the past, he now overindulges in feelings of distrust, unease and aloofness. So he replaces one set of excessive behaviours with another.

Even worse, all this may lead to the musician undermining his own efforts to develop his music, whether by holding back emotionally, by not committing to develop new skills, or by rejecting others' interest and advice. At the extreme the individual may develop a jaundiced view of himself and the world that profoundly injures his progress towards musical mastery. This is why it often takes several lives to get the re-balancing right. Emotional states are complex, and extended effort is required to develop sufficient distance within oneself that one no longer overcompensates.

The final significant point to draw from this musician's case is that dealing with parental rejection exists at the level of the socialised self, yet it simultaneously involves addressing deep level traits. When a life plan involves such a traumatic situation, addressing the socialised self's emotional reactions automatically also involves addressing the associated deep essence traits. However, in such a case the individual needs to resolve his socialised self's feelings about the rejecting parent in order to dive deeper into the inclinations he fostered during previous lives. But because emotionally reacting at the social level is so natural, it may take a number of attempts (that is, a number of lives) for the incarnating individual to learn to deal quickly and effectively with the conditioned socially generated rejection in order to then dive into the deep essence's problematic traits.

An individual with a life goal of rejection fails to make the most of the organised situation when he or she indulges in rejecting others and opportunities without appreciating the positive healing process that underpins rejection. Such individuals may become a mouthpiece for a set of prejudices that they express at every opportunity. Curmudgeons and what are popularly known as "grumpy old men and woman" are public manifestations of the negative expression of rejection. They can be very entertaining. Extremely jaundiced observations often are. But those who have adopted jaundiced rejection as their permanent outlook are literally missing the opportunity of a lifetime.

ACCEPTANCE

The life goals of revaluation, dominance, submission, rejection and acceptance are all manifestations of a spirit's drive to rebalance the way it functions in the human domain. Each incarnating spirit needs to revaluate what, why and how it is doing what it does, often several times during its complete reincarnation cycle. In addition, each spirit needs to learn how to wisely lead and to devotedly follow, and to shift between each as circumstances require. Inevitably spirits also need to adopt either rejection or acceptance to rebalance the way they communicate and interact with other human beings.

Individuals choose a life goal of acceptance when they need to learn to become more open and more accepting of what human existence involves. Learning to accept themselves is an ongoing life lesson for many. But the most obvious reason an incarnating spirit takes on the life goal of acceptance is to rebalance a prior life propensity to judge others, to too readily find fault, to apply strict (and inevitably overly simplistic) measures of behaviour, and to be domineering and controlling in order to "make the world as it should be".

The life goal of acceptance is adopted at different phases of the reincarnation cycle for varying reasons. For example, a spirit in the early stages of its reincarnational cycle has not experienced much, and as a consequence it isn't aware of the nuances of behaviour occurring around it, and has not developed the capacity to respond appropriately to diverse, complex and often messy physical, social, emotional and intellectual inputs. The immature individual's everyday awareness reflects its spirit's lack of experience in the way it uses simplistic moral, religious, legal or common sense schemata in an attempt to control the human messiness it encounters. This desire to control input through an adopted schemata is an entirely natural reaction to human messiness. But when the propensity becomes reinforced over a number of lifetimes, and the drive to order inputs interferes with its experiencing and processing of experiences, then there is a need to "crank it back". Adopting a life goal of acceptance helps the evolving spirit rebalance the deep essence traits of the human psyches it chooses to inhabit.

In the later stages of incarnation, after a spirit has seen it all, there is a natural tendency to step back and leave everyone to it. This may appear to be acceptance. It is not. What the individual is actually doing is avoiding dealing with others' unpleasant manifestations. Learning to accept everyone at all times and in all situations is an entirely different matter. Accordingly, more mature spirits often adopt the life goal of acceptance in order to engage with others and to learn to love them, wholly and unequivocally.

We call this agapè, detached spirit level love. It involves looking past the body and socialised and essence selves in order to perceive the spirit that exists at the core of each individual it encounters. Acceptance in this sense requires clarity. Accepting what you remain unaware of, what you don't perceive, let alone what you don't understand all the consequences of, is not accepting. It is fooling yourself. Many people believe that things are the way they are because God has willed it, or they think that destiny or fate dictates what happens so they conclude they have no choice but to go along with what occurs. This also is not acceptance. It is subservience to a pre-conceived idea of reality. An idea that, incidentally, happens to be wrong.

Acceptance always has its basis in conscious knowing. You see something and accept it. You don't necessarily like it. But you accept it without judgement, without carping, without shaking your head, without self-pity. Individuals need to be inwardly strong to accept in this manner.

The negative manifestation of acceptance is ingratiation, known colloquially as toadying. Toadying is driven by fear. Acceptance that is offered from fear of being exposed, or from fear of being shown to be inadequate, or from fear of not being in control, is ingratiation. It is seeking to be accepted rather than learning to truly accept.

MAINTAINING EQUILIBRIUM

The life goal of maintaining equilibrium is seen most commonly in lives which have a balancing act at their core. Being a politician, television evangelist, head coach of a major sports team, or CEO of a large organisation, offer opportunities to express the life goal of maintaining equilibrium.

By way of explaining what maintaining equilibrium involves, picture a surfer balanced on a wave. The art of surfing is to use the wave's innate energy to ride the board. An experienced surfer is familiar with the conditions commonly present at that beach (the environment) and through repeated rides has learned how the waves behave in various weather conditions (the inputs). So maintaining equilibrium involves becoming familiar with both the environment and the inputs and keeping them all in balance. An experienced surfer is alert to slight changes within the wave and shifts body weight and feet on the board to compensate and so keep the ride going.

Riding a wave is a relatively simple task, as it involves a limited number of inputs, which are easily learned. In contrast, in politics the environment includes numerous agendas and power plays, the daily inputs are many and varied, and the art of riding the wave of public and private support is hugely complex. Falling off the wave in a political environment also has greater consequences. A surfer who falls merely gets wet and can paddle back out to pick up another wave. Politicians who fall may find their political career is over. Political comebacks are complicated and rare.

For this reason any spirit who adopts a life goal of maintaining equilibrium usually needs to practise it for a number of lifetimes. Human interactions are complicated and balancing on any wave that requires the support of other human beings is usually very difficult. Repeated practice is required to be able to work with others and maintain equilibrium.

What commonly happens when an individual first tries maintaining equilibrium is what happens when you first try skateboarding or walking on a high wire: it takes all your effort just to stay upright, let alone move forwards. The result is a state of inertia, in which you remain where you are. In life such individuals may be perceived as self-defensive, as lazy, or as not pushing themselves. Psychologically, they may choose the path of least resistance and to sustain the status quo. Actually, they have to work very hard at staying upright and not falling. In this sense inertia is not a negative behaviour. It merely reflects lack of experience. As the spirit becomes more adept at living with this life goal, and gains more confidence at balancing inputs, the inertia changes to movement.

Riding a wave involves establishing a dynamic equilibrium. The wave itself – whether the wave consists of a belief, an ideal, a discipline, a movement, a vocation, an art form – is on a journey, going somewhere. And the individual is going there too – as long as he or she remains balanced on top of the wave. Riding without falling is a difficult art.

Riding the wave is not for everyone. Many find it too unstable, too dangerous, too frightening. Not being tied to someone, something or somewhere, not having a steady and constant base on which to place one's feet, is too scary for many to handle. But for those who master the art of wave riding it can be addictive. It is not where the wave goes that intoxicates them, but the sheer thrill of riding the wave – and enjoying knowing there is always the danger that they may fall off.

THE LIFE GOAL IN CONTEXT

As we have asserted many times already, a spirit incarnates in a human body in order to evolve. All beings wish to grow. Growth drives the incarnational process. So the life goal of growth, as would be expected, is chosen by almost half the human population at any one time. As we have also attempted to make clear, the majority of the remainder choose the life goals of revaluation, dominance, submission, rejection and submission in order to rebalance themselves and to work on factors that are impeding their growth. Once these have been worked through such individuals usually re-select the life goal of growth – until another limiting factor presents itself and needs to be worked on using the appropriate life goal.

The exception is the life goal of maintaining equilibrium. This ends up having a dual function. Maintaining equilibrium is the life goal that appeals to those we may call natural thrill-seekers. Flying by the seat of their pants, not knowing how things will turn out, being willing to fall and pick themselves up again, only appeals to a particular kind of individual. Most spirits try this life goal at some period during their cycle of incarnations, but it is not their preferred way of engaging with existence in the human domain, which they find difficult enough without deliberately "riding the wave".

However, there is another category of choice with respect to maintaining equilibrium. This is of those who choose this life goal in order to just go with the flow. These people make a minimal effort during their life. If they chose a bland situation to be born into, that life could be very placid and uneventful. They experience little, achieve little, and learn little. Sometimes this option is just what the doctor ordered, insofar as they experienced intense lives previously and they desire a quiet life this time round. At other times it involves keeping a low profile because they have a propensity for big gestures and making lots of noise. For such individuals, keeping a low profile can be as difficult as riding the wave is for others. As we keep repeating, it all depends on what has happened previously, what the spirit wishes to achieve in its next incarnation, and what is the best means for realising that plan.

Each life goal is keyed into a significant life task, choice or series of choices that offer the most appropriate opportunity to experience, learn and develop. The life goal is selected in order to push the life plan to its climax. So if the individual is sufficiently in tune with his or her essence level drives, whenever life throws up a choice, what they choose is an expression of their life goal. In a very real sense, the life goal provides the default position they return to whenever they are lost or confused. Let's now look more specifically at the life plan and the conditions it generates for growth.

CHAPTER 12

The Life Plan and Life Lessons

AS HAS BEEN EXPLAINED, each incarnated spirit has a life plan it selected and organised pre-life. As has also been stated, life plans are complex because they encompass the many interlinked aspects that are involved in facilitating a unique human life and its associated experiences. To recapitulate, this pre-life organisation involves:

- Selecting a body, with its particular genetic disposition and essence traits, along with the cultural conditions into which the body will be born;
- Choosing deep essence traits, positive and negative, from those that the identity has generated during the course of previous incarnations;
- Identifying karmic issues, again drawn from previous incarnations, that will be addressed during the next incarnation;
- Selecting key tasks that address karmic issues and promote essence level growth;
- Organising the conditions for these tasks and key choices to occur;
- Making agreements to meet and be assisted by other individuals, and agreeing to assist others to achieve their aims.

The life plan weaves all these together into a complex mesh. A life goal is then chosen that best fits with what has been planned. The purpose of the life goal is to push the embodied sub-identity back onto task whenever life circumstances throw it off course or divert it into irrelevant side streets.

Ultimately, the purpose behind each life plan is to facilitate the ongoing evolution of a unique spiritual identity. Evolution in turn involves experiencing, processing experiences, learning from them by assimilating lessons, and then using what has been assimilated to identify the next step in further experiencing, processing, learning and assimilating. The over-riding purpose is always to facilitate personal growth.

OPPORTUNITIES FOR GROWTH

Growth is the driver behind everything in the universe. This is seen on Earth where every living creature is born, absorbs food, grows to maturity, ages and dies. This same cycle of growth equally applies to the Earth itself. The Earth was born around four billion years ago. For at least a billion years it absorbed food, in the form of water and trace elements, from the meteors that crashed into its surface. It continues to absorb energy emanating from the Sun. The Earth is a successfully functioning system that is constituted of its interacting lithosphere, hydrosphere, atmosphere and biosphere. As a system it has grown to maturity, as is indicated by the diverse and complex forms of life that exist in the Earth's biosphere.

The Sun and all the planets and moons in this solar system follow the same growth cycle, evolving from simple to complex physical systems. Galaxies similarly grow from small groups – the Local Group contains ten galaxies – to huge clusters containing millions of galaxies.

Finally, there's the universe itself. Born via the big bang, after a few million years the first stars started forming. Billions of years of subsequent growth has resulted in the vast universe of which human beings perceive a minute portion. With the recent scientific confirmation that there are innumerable planets circling countless suns, it is now possible for human beings to appreciate that the universe is teeming with life and species, each of which lives accordingly to its own cycle of birth, feeding, growing to maturity, aging and dying. Growth is endemic to the universe.

In order for an organism to grow it requires conditions that are favourable to growth. A plant requires minerals in its soil, water and sunlight in order to grow to its potential. If any of these are lacking, or are over-abundant, growth is impeded. Similarly, human beings require the right conditions for growth. The physical body needs sufficient food. The socialised self needs language, education, nurturing. The essence self needs opportunities for expression and repeated practice. If any of these are deficient, individuals do not reach their growth potential in this life.

Besides living in conditions that promote growth, two other factors may be identified as necessary for human growth. These are nutrition and digestion. What feeds the human identity? Experiences. The experiences that each individual spirit undergoes during the course of each life, the experiences it has as it lives inside a sub-personality navigating its way from birth to death, provides it with a wide range of experiences. When these experiences are uploaded to the spiritual identity at the end of each life, the spirit is fed by the experiences it has undergone. But in order for those experiences to be nutritious, they have to be digested. Digestion occurs as a result of processing experiences. Processing experiences begins while the spirit is embodied and experiencing the life it has chosen – or been diverted from.

In order to appreciate how the process of digesting experiences occurs, it is useful to consider one's life in the light of lessons. During the course of life each individual has key experiences. These experiences become formative when they are processed and digested. Digestion involves viewing the experience as a life lesson. Indeed, an entire life may be viewed as a series of life lessons. And the more experiences that are digested, the more lessons are learned along the way, and the more successful the life becomes.

LIFE LESSONS

Whenever individuals go through an experience, review it, and come to understand what they did correctly and what incorrectly, that experience becomes a life lesson. Alternatively, if individuals respond to the hassles and problems generated by their experiences by indulging in reactive emotions and by defending their everyday identity through denying, justifying, deflecting or attacking, then it is just another ugly day on Earth.

Tasks and the experiences they generate can be long or short. Equally, life lessons can be extended and many-faceted or brief and singular. Some aims take decades to complete, such as developing a career, and so provide ongoing life lessons. Once a task is completed, such as when one retires from a career, reviewing it can extract further lessons, including perhaps an overall life lesson. On the other hand a life lesson can occur in quite minor situations, when only you realise you didn't do your best, and you resolve to be watchful, not repeat the error, and do better next time the situation recurs.

In this sense any situation can become a life lesson. All it requires is that something nutritious be extracted from it. Life lessons come in many forms and occur in every kind of situation. What they collectively lead to is mastery in whatever field of human endeavour an individual is focused on. Developing physical skills presents many challenges, which must be learnt from in order to reach a high level of achievement. Developing relationship skills requires working on emotional fears and inadequacies and learning to accept and give. Developing intellectual skills requires extended study and improving those aspects of thinking in which one is deficient.

When taking on tasks everyone occasionally fails. By reviewing those failures and deciding what needs to be done better next time, the lesson is learned and the individual develops. Learning and growth are achieved slowly, by increments. Each lesson that is learned, each error that is corrected, each limitation that is broken down, and each negativity that is replaced by its positive opposite, adds to the individual's personal evolution.

LIFE LESSONS AND OBSTACLES

Unfortunately, in general human beings do not learn as much when life goes easily and well. Rather, human beings learn best when they come up against obstacles and problems, when they are confronted by their own limitations and mistakes.

When spiritual identities first begin incarnating in a human body they find their experiences overwhelming. Human life is complex. Being human is difficult. It takes time to develop facility in being a human body's core consciousness. It takes many incarnations to learn to steer the body around, to cope with hormonal tides, to negotiate human social interactions, and to develop personal essence abilities.

For a long time incarnated individuals find other people difficult to figure out. They find themselves difficult to figure out. Others do things they don't understand, for reasons of which they have no comprehension. They themselves do things they don't understand, for reasons they do not comprehend. Understanding is limited. Human existence is complex and relationships are very difficult to negotiate.

In addition, daily life is full of obstacles, any of which may stop individuals in their tracks. Physical obstacles may come in the form of a shortage of money to complete a goal, limited time available to complete a task, a pre-established way of doing things that prevents them form being carried out satisfactorily, or any number of inhibiting factors that prevent an action being accomplished. Sometimes individuals need to face up to the fact that they are just plain inadequate to the task.

In order to overcome obstacles individuals may need to confront their own emotional inadequacy, whether that be in the form of laziness, impatience or ignorance. Emotional obstacles come in the form of lack of communication, misunderstandings, blatant biases, controlling personalities and unarticulated agendas. These need to be overcome using appropriate emotional strategies, such as establishing strong lines of communication, clarifying the issues for everyone involved, diffusing confrontations, and working around those who are fixed in their attitudes.

Intellectual obstacles may include a refusal to acknowledge the facts of a situation, denial of valid research, defence of accepted but outmoded knowledge, and justification for not changing views. These are obstacles that could be addressed by providing a conceptual path between old and new knowledge, by mediating between opposed parties, by demolishing the accepted but incorrect, and by finding ways to facilitate activity.

Each individual perceives obstacles and responds to them in different ways. This difference is mostly due to variations in psychological make-up. Upbringing, social conditioning and whether or not key fears are triggered impact on how an individual responds to a particular obstacle. What is mountainous to one person is barely a bump in the road to another. Then there is whether a particular obstacle is a key or minor part of the life plan.

For each person key obstacles have been organised to arrive at a certain stage in their life in order to provide a specific life lesson. Sometimes these obstacles are so well integrated into daily living that they appear as just another problem to be dealt with. At other times the obstacle arrives from left field and creates a huge disturbance, perhaps sending the individual in a wholly new direction, one they had never previously contemplated. Such is the surprise and joy, or discomfort, or even horror, of incarnated existence.

Clearly, a key contributor to the different ways that people respond to similar obstacles is provided by the life goal. Those with a life goal of growth will respond very differently to those who have a life goal of rejection or of maintaining equilibrium. Yet individuals equally need to process their experiences, review their responses, and draw the lessons. The end outcome is that each person learns new ways of feeling, thinking and doing. As a result, they grow.

Of course, a problem with human beings is that many do not learn from their experiences. They do not learn the lessons. And so they end up repeating the same negative and limiting responses over again. This difficulty is entirely understandable. It is part of the condition of a spiritual identity being incarnated in a human body. Let's now look at that.

CHAPTER 13

The Trade-Offs Of Being Embodied

ENTERING A BODY INVOLVES a number of trade-offs. You gain access to rich experiences ... but that richness is limited by the narrowness of your perceptions. You have the possibility of learning much about the world and about your self ... but many people stay close to what they know, are tentative about exploring new concepts and experiences, and hide behind a narrow band of ideas. And you have the opportunity to gain unique life lessons ... but you forget who you are and why you are here.

FORGETFULNESS

Forgetfulness is arguably the most significant psychological state generated as a result of spiritual identities entering a human body. Forgetfulness is both a necessity and a liability.

Forgetfulness is a necessity because spiritual identities need to forget what they experienced during previous incarnations, forget even that they *are* an embodied spiritual identity, in order to experience their current life in a fresh and open way. If they carried the memory of all their past lives into this life, those past life memories would overwhelm their everyday awareness. Psychologically, they would not be able to experience this life as a new opportunity. Being free to experience anew, to choose anew, to repay and repair and explore anew, requires that individuals do not remember all they have done in the past. That is why forgetfulness is a necessity.

Forgetfulness is a liability because it prevents individuals from remembering why they are living in a particular body, in a specific configuration of physical and social environments, interacting with certain people, living through the experiences they are. With their spiritual core literally out of sight and out of mind, individuals don't appreciate that they can step back and perceive what is happening from a wider experiential perspective.

Because human beings lack a wider context in which to place their current life, they perceive it as the all-in-all of their existence. Forgetting that at their core they are a spirit, they naturally lose themselves in the minutae of their daily experiences. Yet this is advantageous, because if they didn't do so they would not fully engage with their current life and all it entails. Living is experiencing. And experiences provide the nutrition for continued growth.

The disadvantage of forgetfulness is that it naturally leads individuals to ignore inner cues and to forget that there are life tasks to be accomplished life lessons to be learned. Forgetfulness also leads to a loss of focus, as a result of which people turn away from key obstacles instead of confronting them. Then opportunities the individual organised pre-life are ignored and lost.

The two key psychological factors that reinforce forgetfulness are identification and attachment.

IDENTIFICATION

Identification is a state in which an individual's everyday awareness and sense of personal identity is limited to the physical experience of being a body. So while, in reality, each human being consists of a spiritual consciousness using a body to experience life in the physical world, identification leads human beings to think not only that they are a body, but that everyone else they interact with is also a body. The spiritual dimension of identity is forgotten. Instead, identity is seen as synonymous with being a body. This is the state of identification.

Identification leads to two interlinked psychological characteristics. The first is that human beings identify with their body as their self. The second is that everyone identifies with everything they encounter via their body's senses and perceive it as not just wholly real, but as the only real. These two characteristics combine to ensure that a spirit is totally immersed in physical reality. The result is that whatever is experienced in life – whether it be eating breakfast, walking in a park, travelling to work, feeling the rain on one's face, hugging loved ones, feeling accepted, feeling rejected, or experiencing pain – throughout it all one remains "glued" to one's physical experiences and related emotions and thoughts.

Identification, which is the state of awareness being "glued" into physical reality, ensures that you as a spirit don't just observe what happens to the body you occupy, you are fully embedded in your body's experiences. So you, as an embodied spirit, experience what is happening to your current body as happening to you as an identity. If this was not the case, if you did not identify with your body as your self, you would experience your life journey at a remove. It would be like perceiving your life as a movie projected on a screen, rather than experiencing life in the immediate, vivid and intense way you do. Identification makes experiencing real.

ATTACHMENT

Attachment is a by-product of identification. When a spiritual identity identifies with its body as being its self it also naturally becomes attached to the people, objects, places, situations and experiences that form the texture of its daily activities and interactions. These attachments are generated by, and shape, the socialised self. For example, status derives from occupation, level of income, the value of the house lived in, the suburb in which it is situated, and so on. In this way attachments feed the socialised self. And if the individual is wholly identified with their body as being their self, then these attachments contribute much to their sense of self.

Incidentally, this is why individuals are devastated when they lose their job, their expensive house, their highly connected partner, or their prestigious position. Because these things feed their socialised self, and they are intensely invested in and identified with that self, when either job, house, partner or position is removed that person's sense of identity is severely punctured. It can take years to rebuild a new socialised self. From the wider incarnational perspective, it can be seen that what happens is that a spiritual identity becomes invested in the sub-personality generated. It invests in the interaction of its selected body with the social environment in which it lives. Again, as has been stated, this is fine. Being devastated when the socialised self's identity is punctured is all part of the experience of being human.

In fact, people recognise this in the way they adjust their socialised self during the course of growing older. While the formative psychological traits that underpin the socialised self, and therefore everyday identity, usually remain the same throughout a life (only changing if they are worked on), people often change shallow attachments during the course of their life. Not only do they change houses and neighbours, but their taste in clothing, food, music, social activities may change, perhaps significantly. And so their sense of self identity changes accordingly.

Nonetheless, these changes are usually superficial, because individuals' underlying conditioned attitudes, ingrained emotional reactions, and culturally engendered world view remain unaltered. None of this precludes that life experiences, and the lessons learned from them, may lead to radical changes, not only in individuals' attachments and identification but in the way they view themselves. This particularly occurs when an individual emerges from total immersion.

INNER CUES AND EMERGING FROM IMMERSION

Together, forgetfulness, identification and attachments lead to everyday human awareness being totally immersed in the activities of everyday living, as well as in their own inner hormonal, physical, emotional and intellectual responses to those activities. Immersion ensures spirits become, and remain, fully engaged with the experiences that constitute their life.

In general, inner cues impinge into individuals' everyday awareness and are accepted or rejected without reflection. That is, a feeling, impulse or thought appears in a person's awareness regarding what should be done next. While it may involve a big decision, inner cues mostly involve an apparently mundane activity, such as going shopping, or meeting someone for coffee, or even turning right rather than left down a street.

Inner cues come from the individual's own spiritual self, but they are usually not noticed as coming from that source because they merge with all the other feelings, impulses and thoughts that are swirling around within a person's everyday awareness. Such cues may have to do with meeting an individual in order to carry out a pre-life agreement, or starting out down a path that was selected pre-life. Due to individuals' immersion in their life circumstances, the cue often needs to be repeated to attract the individual's attention sufficiently for it to be acted on.

Often, at the time they receive the inner cue, individuals usually don't see it as leading to a momentous turning point in their life. This is because inner cues mesh tightly with the individual's life circumstances and desires, even though some of those desires have actually seeped through, over time, from the spiritual self. So without individuals being aware of it, their everyday awareness has been penetrated by the aims the spirit has set itself for this life. Cues are then acted on without the individual knowing the depth from which they have emanated. In this way even individuals who are not conscious of the spiritual self that pulses at the core of their being end up acting on what they organised pre-life.

Of course, the socialised self can and frequently does interfere with inner cues. Conditioned attitudes often generate doubts. As the individual thinks about the consequences of acting on a cue they start to fear what others will think and doubts rise. Religion also interferes when it has conditioned individuals to hold beliefs that deny the validity of the action urged by the inner cue, or when inculcated religious beliefs undermine individuals' trust in their own spiritual self and its impulses.

In practice, inner cues are a case where a little knowledge can be a dangerous thing. It is often better that an individual accepts a cue without much reflection, or even without any, and just acts on it. This is because once an individual becomes aware of the existence of inner cues all kinds of imaginings, doubts and fantasies emanating from the socialised self can interfere. So it is better to know either nothing, or much more about the process, in order to avoid errors. We'll explore inner cues further in *Mystical Spirituality*.

For now the point needs to be made that while a spirit's total immersion in the activities of daily life are what human existence is all about, it is also possible, in a sense, to lift one's head out the stream, to no longer be completely immersed, to look around, and become more aware of the processes and decisions that give a life journey its particular flavour. In particular, one can gain greater awareness of the life plan that one has chosen this time round.

Why do so? Why wish to perceive and learn more? The answer is, in order to achieve more in this life. And especially to diminish, to some extent at least, the hit and miss quality of everyday existence that leads most individuals to fulfil only a small percentage of what they set out to achieve.

CHAPTER 14

Incarnation and Growing to Maturity

EVERYONE CAN CHOOSE A LIFE that is full or a life that is empty. That choice can be made pre-life or while living the selected life. Nothing is set in stone or unable to be changed. Aspects of a life plan, even the entire life plan, can be jettisoned at any stage. Indeed, some people become so immersed in their body and its social conditions, or in the work in which they are engaged, and as a consequence enjoy their life experience so much, that they miss a number of pre-organised opportunities. And they, in fact, are content to do so.

It is natural for individuals to seek personal fulfilment and satisfaction. That is as it should be. There are many ways to learn, and nothing that is experienced is lost. Any experience can provide a life lesson, including those that arise accidentally, as a by-product of opportunities not accepted. Because other opportunities always arrive. That is the condition of incarnation. Nonetheless, there is a natural developmental process involved in a spirit's series of incarnations. And, after a considerable number of incarnations, the spirit naturally becomes curious about what exactly is occurring "behind" its life journey. This is the situation when deeper perceptions manifest in the everyday awareness. These usually emanate from the energetic or spiritual levels.

For example, an individual may recognise another person at a deep level, perhaps through an inexplicably strong attraction or repulsion, which suggests that the person is previously known to them, and not during this life. An individual may have the feeling that they have been here before, either in a particular place, or just feel generally that they have had a body previously. Perhaps they possess essence skills that they did not have to work hard to develop, which are superior to those possessed by others around them, and which do not appear to have been inherited genetically. Perhaps they experience a sense of obligation or responsibility to another that doesn't make sense to anyone else among their family or friends, or in terms of what has occurred during this life.

These, and many other feelings, carry intimations that life is not as it appears to be. And as these feelings grow, that is, as they manifest more frequently and more strongly within the everyday awareness, individuals start to become curious, not only about these feelings, but also about the nature of human existence in general. They start wanting to emerge from complete immersion in life experiences. And as part of this process they naturally seek answers to questions regarding the nature of their existence. This questioning is a reflection of growing maturity.

GAINING MATURITY

As a general and somewhat simplistic statement, we can say that children play and adults work. Children are supported by their parents, by other family members, or by the state as they obtain an education and learn to function in a culture, responding to its social restrictions and taking advantage of the opportunities it provides. Adults earn a living, support themselves and perhaps others, including children, share what they have, work to achieve their aims, all the while struggling to achieve those aims.

The same developmental process applies spiritually. Those who are just starting out on their sequence of incarnations need support. They struggle to look after themselves. They play a great deal as they immerse themselves in the joys and terrors of being incarnated. Over time individuals become socialised and learn to function with others. They then start developing essence level skills, which result from being attracted to certain lifestyles, certain ways of living, and certain levels of doing, feeling or thinking. They work on skills and develop their abilities in selected fields of human endeavour. Eventually, over a series of incarnations, if they are so inclined, they develop mastery. Having higher level abilities, expertise or mastery, they are then in a position to assist others in their struggles to similarly gain expertise in those same fields of endeavour. All this reflects growing maturity as a spirit incarnating in a series of human bodies.

As observation confirms, no single individual gains mastery over *all* the innumerable fields of human interaction, expertise and knowledge. But it is certainly possible to gain mastery over many. It all depends on individuals' inclinations, which in turn reflect the impulses of their core disposition. It also depends on how much effort individuals make during the course of multiple incarnations. As observation also makes clear, some people make much more of an effort than others.

However, no matter what fields of expertise in which an individual chooses to develop mastery, there is one kind of expertise that every single incarnated spirit has to address. This is the art of reincarnation. Ultimately, growing maturity as an incarnating spirit is reflected in a continued questioning of the nature of existence, a deepening knowledge of one's own self, and a broadened understanding of human psychospiritual make-up. Yet this maturity doesn't just collect like rain in a puddle. Effort is required. Maturity is hard won. Why? Because much in the lower levels of the five-layered self doesn't need or want this effort.

Children are ignorant of the wider world around them. In contrast, adulthood involves becoming more aware of what is occurring in the world and being more responsible for it. There is much in each human being that is childish and ignorant. And just as some children are fun and loving and others are nasty and spiteful, so there are parts of the layered self that are fun and loving, and others that are nasty and spiteful. These latter parts, along with those parts that are blissfully ignorant, need to be expunged, while the playful and loving parts need to be nurtured and matured so that the individual, in all parts, becomes knowing and responsible. The maturing process involves development, purification and clarity.

DEVELOPMENT

When individuals are born their centres do not automatically function to their full potential. Just like the physical body, the centres grow. And just as the physical body needs the right kind of sustenance in order to grow to its adult potential, so the three essence level centres requires nourishment in order to develop to their potential. What nourishes them is the energy directed into them when they are used on a daily basis.

The development of the centres reflects the stages of the body's growth. So they can be considered to grow from infant, through child and teen, to adult. Infants grapple with the task of connecting with and utilising their moving, emotional and intellectual centres. Children learn through playing and also start to realise that what they do, feel and think impacts on others. Teens develop personal interests and begin to flex their moving, emotional and intellectual muscles. And adults function proficiently and responsibly in their moving, emotional and intellectual centres. As can easily be observed, just because an individual is older than twenty-one does not mean they are a fully functioning adult.

Individuals who are adult in all parts of their essence self will be able to function with proficiency in each centre's three constituent parts. This means that an adult in the emotional centre will process and respond to physical forms, empathise emotionally and experience love, and be able to think intuitively. An adult in the moving centre will move and work efficiently with the moving part of the their moving centre, will experience the instinctive and adrenaline emotions but will not live in their negative manifestations, and will be able to solve practical problems. An adult in the intellectual centre will keep formatory thought in proportion, be open to awe and a sense of scale and not be engaged in justifying negativities, and will be able to think abstractly to develop an overview of their life journey.

Adult development involves the ability to use the centres appropriately. So when one is faced with a practical problem, the moving centre is used to solve it rather than emoting or logically analysing it. In practice, this means adults are able to turn their centres on and off at will. Many people struggle to do this because their natural preference for one centre means they tend to use it in all situations, whether it is appropriate or not. So emotional types commonly emote when faced with a moving centre problem, and intellectual types try to intellectualise themselves out of an emotional problem.

Overall, the essence self's development results in an individual maturing in each centre from infant to adult, and establishing an appropriate and working balance between the activities of the three centres. Without essence maturity individuals remain at a low level of moving, emotional and intellectual functioning. And without balance between the centres they are incapable of switching at will between centres and using each appropriately.

All this understandably requires considerable focus, dedication and application. It is a process that takes multiple incarnations. What aids essence level development is when individuals initiate an interest or skill and concentrate on it, whether it be gardening, nursing, art-making, building, teaching, and so on. These types of interests, which for many may also become an occupation, provide a context in which moving, emotional and intellectual skill sets are developed. It is what the individual brings to each task, perhaps more than the nature of the task itself, that facilitates essence development.

What retards developing the centres and achieving balance between them? Negativity in actions, emotions and thoughts.

NEGATIVITIES

The problem with negativities is that they interrupt the proper functioning of the three centres. Negativities distend the centres, preventing them from achieving their full potential.

Negativities impact on each of the biological, social and essence levels. The impact of conditioning and trauma on a growing child was discussed in Chapter Five, along with the fact that individuals utilise psychological mechanisms to cope with either trauma or the stressful conditions of everyday life. These coping mechanisms distend the centres. The ways formative experiences shape the human psychology are relevant to any discussion of negativities. So is the discussion of "the stuff in basement" that was initiated in *Experimental Spirituality*.

To begin with the biological self, negativities may impact on the biological self in a purely physical sense. An individual may have an accident during childhood that injures the spine, as a result of which the moving part of the moving centre will never function at its full capacity. Chemical imbalances in the biological self, along with genetic dispositions, can impede the functioning of the emotional and intellectual centres. In most, but not all cases, the dysfunction was selected before the life began, to provide an opportunity to experience human existence from a narrowed perspective. There are many possible reasons for this. Some reasons are karmic, with the individual needing to experience the same type of limitation to which they had previously condemned others. Some reasons are psychological, with the individual wrestling with a particular aspect of the bodily-socialised-essence self configuration and requires limited functioning in order to do so.

Negative emotions and attitudes impede the full functioning of the emotional centre. Continued negative experiences, or brief but powerful traumatic events, distend the emotional centre and generate habitual defensive behaviours and conditioned reactions that run counter to essence level emotional development. It is extremely rare for a human being not to experience, during their formative years, various kinds of negative emotional inputs. There are traumatic childhood events, which may include domestic violence, emotional, physical or sexual abuse, the death of family members, the drag of poverty, and parents' negative behaviour towards their children. The wider community or culture may also present an oppressive, threatening or fear-inducing environment, which not only limits the development of social skills but inhibits the growth of essence abilities. Comment has been made that many cultures today still consider females to be second-class citizens, so education is withheld from them and they are treated as the playthings of men and their elders. Yet another factor is the trauma generated by negative physical environments, where famine, war and poverty create conditions that impact negatively on the growing child's emotional centre.

One way people cope with traumatic events is through repressing them. This creates "stuff in the basement", consisting of repressed memories, trauma and fears. As long as individuals do not experience similar situations in later life they get through daily situations okay. But when an event occurs that too closely echoes what they went through when younger, that event triggers repressed emotions, the door to the basement opens, and the repressed feelings and thoughts roar up into everyday awareness. Actions carried out under the influence of the stuff that has poured up out of the basement can harm everyone involved.

Finally, there is the way that negative concepts are conditioned into individuals, creating thought tracks in their intellectual centre that in later years are automatically followed. Culturally, conditioned ideas have plagued humanity through the millennia. History is full of fantasies regarding goblins or trolls in the woods, werewolves and witches in the night, and monsters under the bed. It is easy for contemporary humanity to laugh at this as childish silliness. However, many current concepts are equally as fantastical and are as fervently believed in, including racism, sexism, casteism and social prejudices of all kinds. Many believe in heaven and hell or in the idea that competition will create the best of possible worlds. Traditional religious theologies, reductive scientific theories, and plain human ignorance (maintained by denying known facts) limit the ability of humanity as a whole to utilise its intellectual capacity to its full potential. When such limited thinking is projected into the intellectual centre of a growing child the result is a sticky web of fallacious thinking that, at best, takes years for the adult to extract him or herself from – if that happens at all.

In summary, negativity takes three major forms: repressed trauma lurking in the basement of each individual's psychological make-up; defensive and coping behaviours individuals use to protect themselves from real and imagined threats during the course of everyday living; and cultural and social conditioning that envelop all in a general negative haze.

Of course, not all family upbringing, cultural and social conditioning, and childhood experience is negative. Most individuals receive positive support during their childhood, which takes the form of education, personal guidance and individuals who function as role models. Together, these aid socialization and stimulate essence development. Nonetheless, in order to become adult in the three centres each person needs to eliminate, short-circuit, transform or transcend all negativities. Naturally, it is too much to do so in one lifetime, especially when there is stuff in the basement of the deep essence, generated in previous incarnations, that remains unresolved.

As far as this current life is concerned, if any individual is able to resolve key formative experiences through an extended exercise of recognising how they occurred, processing their impact on one's psychological make-up, forgiving others who are involved, forgiving oneself, dismantling negative coping mechanisms, and correcting the resulting distended functioning within the three centres, doing so would be a major achievement. A fuller discussion of this process of inner healing and development will be offered in the next book in this series, *Psychological Spirituality*.

For now we will deal with two other aspects that facilitate essence growth. These are clarity and purification.

CLARITY

Clarity, purification and development occur hand-in-hand. Clarity is required because it helps identify the negativities that are impacting on essence level functioning, while purification eliminates those negativities so further development may take place. In this way, clarity, purification and development are bound up in the process of inner growth and spiritual evolution.

The purpose of clarity is to identify limiting negative behaviours. Merely perceiving yourself correctly – without being defensive, and without giving in to conditioned assumptions about yourself and how you are viewed by others – is a major undertaking. By adulthood the socialised self and the everyday identity it feeds are crystallised. Achieving clarity about this crystallised identity, and appreciating how it functions during the course of everyday living, is a difficult task. It involves standing outside one's own psychological functioning and observing it in action.

This activity itself is potentially traumatic, because it requires you to view your everyday identity – the identity you have invested in your whole life as being your self – as not being your self. In that case, what is your self? On the human level, it is your essence self. Achieving clarity involves using the essence self's intellect as an observer to collect data about your everyday identity and its behaviour. Once you have the data you can process it. The processing is carried out by the essence self as a whole.

Clarity applies on multiple levels. First there is the task of gaining clarity with respect to the momentum of your everyday identity (see Chapter Six). This involves examining your culture, roles, routines, habitual behaviours and conditioned reactions, and identifying how much of your world view, general life outlook, preferred and avoided social roles, and the habits and reactions in which you are invested are the result of conditioning rather than being chosen. In particular, the negative and self-limiting aspects of these five factors need to be identified and processed before those that are perceived as negative may be purified out of your everyday identity.

Next is the task of becoming clear about the nature of your biological and socialised selves. This is so negative psychological traits may be eliminated – or, if this is not possible, at least minimised so the essence self may function with minimal impediments.

The essence self itself also needs to be observed and clarity gained with respect to its functioning, and insight gained regarding the limiting and negative traits that are impeding inner growth. Examples include negative instinctive and moving centre behaviours such as eating disorders, sexual dysfunction, and addictions, plus adrenaline emotions that spill over into bullying or domestic violence. Negativities in the emotional centre include guilt, self-pity, resentment, ongoing anger, insecurity, inner considering (dwelling on how hard done by one is), fear of rejection or exposure, intimidating others, manipulating others, and so on. Negativities in the intellectual centre include operating with fixed attitudes (drawing on conditioned, prejudicial and judgemental views), using the intellect to deny the reality of situations and facts, and holding fast to doctrines and beliefs that range from the intellectually dishonest to the outright pathological.

Only once clarity is gained is it possible to begin purifying one's psychological make-up. Psychologically, clarification and purification are a step-by-step process, requiring focus on single aspects of the psychological make-up. Yet everything in the human psychology is linked, so with effort sustained over time these single aspects combine to address a significant portion of an individual's entire psychological make-up.

PURIFICATION

Purification consists of three steps. First is gaining clarity about what is holding you back. This requires you to observe the activities of your everyday identity as it goes about its daily living and identifying limiting and negative factors and behaviours. Second is eliminating those factors and behaviours that distend the essence self and limit growth. This involves replacing negative emotions and attitudes with positive emotions and attitudes. Third is shifting the focus of the everyday awareness from the activities of the body and the socialised self onto the essence self.

Shifting focus to the essence self enables more daily time, energy and effort to be spent on moving, emotional and intellectual activities rather than on the socialised self's coping and defence mechanisms. This process may be thought of as a withdrawal from external life that results in a degree of isolation in the midst of everyday living, but in fact it merely involves acknowledging the presence of one's inner resources and devoting more time and energy to nurturing them. By withdrawing from otherwise negative socially conditioned activities that engage you both externally and internally you become freed up to spend more time developing your essence potential.

There is no easy way to purify the layered self of negativities. They are numerous. Some run very deep, lifetimes deep. Accordingly, purification is an ongoing process that requires constant effort and vigilance. However, some traits, even major ones that loom very large in the everyday awareness, can be all but eliminated with a short concentrated burst of focused effort. On the other hand, those that function at a low level and so do not attract much attention within may carry on for years.

However, just the activity of observing negativities and understanding how they became lodged in your psychology takes the sting out of many of them. This is because clarity involves stepping back from incessant engagement with one's everyday self and, from the perspective of the essence self's intellect, seeing it as only one aspect of oneself, and a small aspect at that. This act of stepping back is itself partly purifying. Just knowing a behaviour is not intrinsic to one's identity, and that one no longer needs to invest in it as being an essential part of oneself, can be a huge relief.

This chapter has aimed to indicate how the three steps of development, clarity and purification occur together, as three aspects of the single process of gaining maturity. An example will show how this works in practice and take us into the next topic, mastering the art of incarnation.

PART THREE

MASTERING THE ART OF INCARNATION

CHAPTER 15

How A Life Plan Manifests

HOW INDIVIDUALS MASTER THE ART of incarnation may be understood by first appreciating that all the factors identified so far fit together and contribute to a life plan. This may be best explained through an example.

Let's say a man, who we will call Bill, works for an engineering company in the position of overseer. In this position he has to quality check the work of others. As far as Bill's bosses are concerned he manages quality control more than competently. But how he performs the role personally and psychologically is actually not smooth because his fellow workers find Bill overbearing. He nitpicks their work, finding fault where they consider there is little or none. As a result Bill's fellow workers consider him to be a pain in the arse.

Let's further say that Bill is dedicated to practising what is being advocated here. So he starts examining himself. And, in a moment of clarity, one day he sees himself as the overbearing nitpicker that his fellow workers perceive him to be. This observation of himself was always available to him, of course. But in general people defend their everyday identity. So previously, whenever a co-worker bit back over his nitpicking, to himself Bill justified being overbearing on the grounds that otherwise quality would fall. Or he deflected and said he was just doing his job. Or he denied that he was being overbearing at all, arguing that his co-workers needed to harden up, learn to take criticism, and stop whinging. To others he attacked those who complained, saying they were just being lazy. Whatever way Bill had previously defended his everyday identity, he suddenly has a moment of clarity and sees how he behaves.

Next Bill processes the observation by tracing the source of his behaviour back to his childhood. His father was a very dominating parent. He pushed Bill throughout his school years, demanding ever higher marks. And he instilled in Bill the attitude that he always needed to do better than anyone else in his class or in whichever school sports team he played. To others, the boy Bill was indeed successful. But he was actually driven by a feeling of inadequacy. Years of his father telling him he needed to do better had instilled in him a self-image that he wasn't good enough. So when he was appointed overseer at the engineering company his feelings of inadequacy, underpinned driven also by a fear of failure, led him to become overbearing and push everyone more than required, just as his father had done to him.

Other people who knew both father and son might have commented on how the domineering and overbearing father lived on in the son. But what they couldn't see was what Bill now came to understand, which was that his father's upbringing had instilled in him a fear of being inadequate, and that his father was actually driven himself by the same fear. Apparent external strength was undermined by inner weakness.

Appreciating all this, Bill is now is a position to address his overbearing behaviour. Because all socially manifested behaviour has its source in inward self-image and emotional attitude, Bill needs to change inwardly. Only then will his overbearing outward behaviour change. So he eliminates his feelings of inadequacy by acknowledging to himself that he is no longer a child, no longer needs his father's approval, and that he is perfectly capable of doing the job he has been appointed to. Accordingly, he makes a conscious effort to replace all words of criticism with words of praise and to address any situation in which work is not up to specification not by being overbearing but by helping the worker to achieve the required standard. Nitpicking has become a habitual behaviour, so each day he also has to watch himself to ensure he doesn't slip back into his everyday identity's tendency to nitpick.

Bill's bosses don't notice any change. The standard of work Bill oversees maintains the same high level. But for Bill the feeling involved in producing it is very different. He no longer performs the role of overseer in a negative emotional state. He's more relaxed inside himself. His co-workers are less stressed, and as a consequence start enjoying coming to work each day.

In the course of seeing, processing, addressing and changing a negative behaviour, Bill has used clarity, purification and inner development to become more mature emotionally. In the process he has also cracked part of his crystallised everyday identity. Better adjusted in his socialised self, he now utilises a deeper and positive part of his essence self.

GOING DEEPER

But let's say Bill doesn't stop here. Let's say he continues considering what was involved in his childhood upbringing. Observing other everyday behaviours related to his being overbearing, he realises that he hates being criticised. And he has a response of lashing out at others verbally when he feels that he is being unfairly picked on.

What Bill now realises is that this behaviour of verbally lashing out is a result of conditioning. When young and he felt dominated by his father, he didn't lash out because his cultural conditioning was to respect his father, an attitude his father instilled in him. So while anger and resentment bubbled up inside him, and he wanted to lash out at times, he repressed his emotions, which included both the anger and the desire to lash out. The result is that in adulthood, whenever anyone pushes the wrong button by criticising or attacking him, he gives them a verbal lashing. The problem is that criticism takes him back to his childhood experiences of when his father repeatedly made him feel inadequate. To avoid re-experiencing that criticism, and feeling the associated pain, he lashes out and attacks.

Then he starts thinking about those repressed feelings. Using the concepts presented here, Bill comes to realise that he has a core disposition of warrior. In addition, his modality is a blend of expressive and inward. This leads him to enjoy interacting with others, but he is also naturally self-reflective. The downside is that he is more disposed to internalise his feelings than to physically strike out, a readiness that has been reinforced by his dominating father's upbringing.

The flip side is that as a warrior he is naturally drawn towards challenges. So during his childhood, despite his father making him feel inadequate, he never gave up. Where some would have become totally passive and fallen into despair, or others would have acquiesced and sought to make their father happy, Bill saw his childhood situation as a challenge. All this was at a subconscious level, of course, below the level of his everyday awareness. So he always tried his best, but this was only partially to make his father happy. More it was because he enjoyed pushing himself.

Having thought through all this, Bill now understands that there has been a conflict between his warrior spirit and his socialised self. His warrior spirit embraces challenges, whereas his socialised self has developed a self-image of inadequacy. The result is inner conflict. During his early childhood, when he remained dependent on his parents, and when the formation of his socialised self dominated his everyday awareness, Bill's warrior spirit was limited to expressing itself in the way that he refused to give up. But during his mid-teens, when his socialised self had largely reached its adult form but had not yet completely crystallised, Bill frequently felt an inner drive to break free. This manifested in a desire to leave his parents' home. In psycho-spiritual terms, this conflict was between his socialised self, which constantly pulled him back into conforming to his father's desires, and his spiritual core consciousness which was giving him inner cues that urged him to move away and seek freedom.

This urge was further supported by his life goal, that of growth. During his teens Bill had often felt confused, muddled. But by the age of eighteen the inner cues impinging on his everyday awareness, backed by the life goal of growth, were sufficient to propel him to leave home.

An immediate consequence was that Bill now needed to support himself. So he discontinued his education. Being a moving-emotional type, he enjoyed working with his hands. So he joined an engineering company, underwent further training, and rose in the business. Bill's father saw this decision as further proof that his son was inadequate and not up to his own high standards. But leaving home was a significant turning point in Bill's life, in which, without knowing it, he was responding to inner cues from his spiritual self that suggested what he had to do in order fulfil his warrior drive.

Having appreciated all this, Bill now reached another key turning point in his life. He had always been drawn to distant countries, especially mountainous areas. He had often tramped in the mountains of his own country, but he had done little travelling overseas. In his forties he now decided that he needed a new challenge. So he applied for a job constructing railways and bridges in a distant country. The new company he joined appreciated his expertise, enthusiasm and positivity.

After shifting countries, inside himself he was no longer frustrated. He had overcome his socialised self's fear of inadequacy. And each day he experienced the warrior bliss of meeting new challenges. He also made new friends. But one man in particular he felt instantly attracted to. In fact, Bill and his new friend had made a mutual pre-life agreement to meet and together pursue their bliss. As a result they established an engineering company. Naturally, having known each other in previous lives, there was emotional baggage, carried in their deep essence, which they each needed to work through. But that is another story.

OBSTACLES AND THE LIFE PLAN

What this example makes clear is the significance of obstacles. Bill's upbringing provided an obstacle he needed to confront and overcome in order to express his inner nature and fulfil his life plan. It was the inner conflict and frustration caused by his socialised self grating against his warrior disposition that led him to seek change, to hear his spirit's inner cues, and to achieve a fulfilling life. If he had remained cowered by his father's conditioning, and had never faced up to the self-limiting negativity of his socialised self, he would have failed to achieve what he had set himself in this life.

Of course, it would not have been a failed life. Far from it. He still would have had experiences and the opportunity to gain life lessons from them. However, he would not have lived the life he intended. He would not have met the friend with whom he had set up a business as per their pre-life agreement. He would not have learned the specific lessons he, as an ongoing spiritual identity, had decided he needed to learn in order to further evolve. And he very likely would not have found his bliss.

Obstacles are a necessary part of developing and growing. As such most major life obstacles are pre-organised as part of the life plan. Obstacles complexify and intensify life experiences. They present problems that need to be resolved. And they bring to a head inner conflicts individuals need to work through in order to mature as spiritual beings.

In Bill's case, obstacles brought him to a turning point. He realised he needed to change his behaviour. In doing so he was able to break the shackles of his socialised self, crack the habitual behaviour of his everyday identity, and engage with his essence self. In the course of opening himself up internally he stopped listening to his fears and made it easier for his spiritual self to give him inner cues.

The obstacle generated by his father's dominance was a key early phase of Bill's life plan. The father-son relationship was, naturally, an agreement made pre-life between two spirits. The relationship was an experience each needed in order to address their own deep essence traits. Working through this particular obstacle led Bill on to fulfil the consequent phases of his life plan.

Everyone has the opportunity and ability to fulfil their own life plan in this way. This is the process we are calling mastering the art of incarnation. It is a process that requires individuals to look at themselves unblinkingly and acknowledge their inadequacies.

CHAPTER 16

Confronting Negativities

NOTHING IN LIFE PREPARES YOU for the shock of standing back and seeing yourself for the first time as a flawed human being. Nothing prepares you for the discomfort, the distaste, that is engendered when you see your negativities operating in full bloom. Nothing compensates for the realisation that you are far less than you have long imagined yourself to be as you lived cocooned in the conditioned world that your everyday self occupies.

This is because, as has been made clear earlier, much in the everyday self is a crystallisation of the psychological defence mechanisms developed during the childhood and teenage years. When these defensive behaviours crystallise, which typically occurs by twenty one, individuals not only accommodate themselves to those behaviours, they become very comfortable with them. This is so even when profoundly disturbing negativities are embedded deep in their psychological make-up. The reason individuals accommodate themselves to negativities is that familiarity breeds comfort. Repeated exposure to conditioned psychological behaviours, attributes and traits leads individuals to accept even the worst as having a place within their layered self.

Of course, this acceptance need not be the case. But in order for it not to be so, individuals have to confront the negative aspects of their psychology. Such a confrontation involves not just observing those traits, but owning them. However, this is such an intense, outright scary proposition that most people find it easier and more comforting to live with the devil they know than wrestle that devil into submission. And so they end up making excuses for negative traits within their make-up rather than casting them out.

The approach to psychospiritual development advocated here, in which an individual overcomes inner obstacles in order to evolve as a spiritual identity, is predicated on observing, owning up to, understanding and eliminating one's negativities. Why? Because negativities limit the functioning of the layered self's positive attributes and inhibit growth towards maturity. So the task of mastering the art of incarnation necessarily involves addressing the negative aspects of your everyday identity. And deeper.

It could be said that while the first driver of spiritual growth consists of the individual's own fanned intention to do all it takes to evolve spiritually, the second driver is addressing all those factors that inhibit such growth by confronting negative, self-limiting traits. As previously noted, negativities take many forms and exist in all layers of the self. At this point it is not necessary to detail them. This will be done in *Psychological Spirituality*. For now it is sufficient to make a general observation that locates the task of confronting negativities within the broader task of mastering the art of incarnating. We'll start with the need for courage.

BEING COURAGEOUS

Spiritual endeavours are not often thought of as requiring courage. But being courageous is a necessary preliminary to confronting one's limitations. Without courage, how will you do it? We commented that confronting one's negativities is a scary activity. The truth is that the everyday self's defence mechanisms usually stop an individual from confronting briefly glimpsed negative and self-limiting behaviours, because as soon as the glimpse occurs defensiveness automatically kicks in and either denial, self-justification, deflection or attack promptly represses the observation and buries it.

However, in a quiet hour, away from the hurly-burly of daily life, when one's socialised self is not engaged in the never-ending task of defending itself, it is entirely possible for one's essence self to remember that glimpse and to start wondering about it, where it came from, how often such glimpses manifest, what they reveal, and so on. In this way the particular negative behaviour can be considered in a low-key, detached fashion, without engaging the everyday self's usual defensive sturm and drang.

This first step is in itself a courageous act. It involves glimpsing one's negative self in operation and subsequently mulling over it in order to understand one's behaviour. The second step involves observing the same behaviour on other occasions, then analysing them all in order to understand the negativity's source. This similarly requires courage. As does the third step, that of taking up the task of purification by confronting negative behaviours and working to eliminate them.

The example of Bill given in the previous chapter will make this process clearer. We noted that one day Bill saw himself as the overbearing nitpicker that his fellow workers perceived him to be. In the terms we are now discussing, he obtained a glimpse of his everyday identity's negative behaviour.

There are two principle ways such a glimpse may be generated. Sometimes an inner cue is sent by the spiritual self and is perceived in the everyday awareness. In Bill's case the result was that he saw what he previously had not. The second way the glimpse occurs is when others say so. Such statements are colloquially called home truths. Friends and family have the opportunity to become very aware of one's weaknesses and failings. Sometimes, such as during truth-telling sessions around the dinner table, one person may quietly communicate their observations to another close to them. But more commonly home truths are spoken during arguments or in moments of intense emotion. Of course, the person making the statement usually does so to attack another in order to defend their own everyday self. But the fact that such observations are often uttered in self-defence does not invalidate their applicability.

Whether a glimpse you have of your own behaviour results from another's observation or via an inner cue, the big question is whether you are willing to take it on board and act on it. Are you sufficiently courageous to confront your personal limitations, see them as obstacles to growth, and dismantle them? The answer to this question may be thought of in terms of momentum.

In Bill's case, his glimpse of his nitpicking behaviour came via an inner cue. Immediately he received this glimpse, the momentum of his socialised self kicked in and sought to swamp him by manifesting defensiveness. However, that defensive momentum was opposed by the momentum of his life plan, which itself was driven by his life goal of growth.

This opposition of momentums applies to every single individual. Everyone has a crystallised everyday identity laced with defensive behaviours that automatically strive to keep awareness immersed in the flow of reactions to daily living. On the other hand, everyone also has a life goal that pushes them towards carrying out their self-selected life tasks and realising their life plan.

So the question is: Which momentum are you following? The momentum of crystallised everyday identity operating at the level of your socialised self? Or the momentum of the essence self, driven by the life goal, as it works to realise the tasks selected pre-life by your spiritual self?

Bill had the courage to accept the glimpse he received from his spiritual self and utilise it. Subjectively, from the perspective of his everyday awareness, this first led to a new life perspective, then to new life possibilities opening up for him. Objectively, from the perspective of his spiritual self, it can be said that he switched from the momentum of his everyday identity to the momentum of his essence self, using its psychologically embedded life goal to realise his pre-designed life plan.

Of course, changing momentums is never as simple as this. In practice, striving individuals regularly switch back and forth between the momentum of the everyday self and the momentum of the essence self and its life goal. There is nothing wrong with this changing of momentums. Everyone has periods when they forget their essence tasks and become immersed in, and reactive to, the circumstances of everyday life. Then they re-awake, re-orient themselves, and go back to consciously working on their life tasks. However, with sustained application the sleeping periods become shorter and the waking periods longer.

The aim of spiritual becoming is that the life plan and its associated life goal so infuse one's everyday awareness that everyday life becomes directed towards fulfilling one's self-selected life tasks. This is a possibility for everyone who strives to engage with their spiritual self, no matter how many times they have incarnated and what their level of maturity. And it all begins with courageously taking up what one discovers, is told or is given.

The next question is: How does one build and sustain this courage?

SUSTAINING COURAGE

Courage is a by-product of a change in attitude. Changes in attitude occur as a series of steps in the process of striving to achieve spiritual maturity.

For Bill, the first change in attitude was being willing to give up the normal overwhelming attachment to his everyday socialised identity and to accept criticism of that self. It involved being willing to give up defending his everyday self. The second change in attitude was being willing to analyse his behaviour and attempt to figure out where it came from. And the third change in attitude was being willing to adjust his normal behaviours. Or at least, those behaviours that had to do with his overbearing nitpicking.

It could said that the first step is the most difficult. This is because once one is willing to step out of one's defensiveness and accept criticism of one's self, the other two steps of analysis and changing behaviours reasonably follow. But without having the courage to take the first step the other two are not possible. As just noted, the courage to take that first step occurs as a result of one either consciously or subconsciously realising that there is another path and another momentum that one's life might follow.

TURNING POINTS AND INITIATING CHANGE

In Chapter Six, the term turning point was used to describe a key moment in an individual's life journey when everyday identity and its repeated negative behaviours are glimpsed and, after analysing that perception, a decision is made to change life direction.

Turning points usually occur when an individual gets sick of doing the same things the same way, over and over. One popularly acknowledged turning point is the mid-life crisis, even though it frequently results in only superficial change. A conversion experience is another example of a time in life when individuals decide to turn their life around. The emotions associated with turning points include unhappiness, dissatisfaction, frustration, boredom and self-disgust. Those who have decided to change their life often think it was unhappiness or boredom or frustration that caused them to do so. In fact, such emotions are symptoms, not causes. The underlying cause for individuals deciding that their life has reached a turning point, and that they need to change their life profoundly, is that they have recognised and engaged with the momentum of their life plan.

Accordingly, it may be said that a turning point is a key moment in a life, when individuals switch from being driven by their socialised everyday self and instead engage with their life plan as enacted by their essence self, which in turn is driven by its psychologically embedded life goal.

This is what happened with Bill. He reached just such a turning point. As a result he changed the momentum of his life, engaged with his life plan, and went on to previously unthinkable experiences, such as travelling overseas, meeting his old (that is, his pre-life) friend, and going into business with him.

In all this the courage Bill had to confront his negative behaviour can be seen to be a by-product of his deeper urge, emanating from his spiritual self, to realise his life plan. Listening to the inner cues emanating from his spiritual self initiated a profound change in attitude. As a result he disengaged from his socialised self and its defensive modes of behaviour. Having disengaged, he then created space inside himself for his essence-level life goal of growth to manifest in his everyday awareness. And it was by accepting the drive towards growth that he accomplished all that he subsequently did.

CONFRONTING ONE'S SELF

We conclude all we have discussed here by observing that the process of self-confrontation is ongoing. There are so many aspects to the layered self, full as it is of numerous self-limiting behaviours, attitudes and traps arrayed within the biological, socialised and essence selves, that it takes lifetimes to ferret them all out and eliminate them. It takes lifetimes because it took lifetimes to put them in there in the first place. Courage to do so comes when one takes up the challenge offered by glimpses into one's inner nature, when one fans that glimpse into a turning point, and when one makes the commitment to transform one's life.

First comes the glimpse. Next comes a change in attitude, a change that is itself a manifestation of the inner desire, emanating from the spiritual self, to realise the life plan. Realising the life plan involves changing the momentum of one's life from that supplied by the socialised everyday self to that provided by the essence self. Courage is a natural by-product of both the desire to change, cued by the spiritual self, and the momentum to realise the life plan that is driven by the essence self and its life goal. In this way it can be seen that attitude, momentum and courage reinforce one another.

So you don't first need courage in order to transform your life. Changing your attitude, which means having the genuine intention to change yourself is sufficient. Then, as the deeper levels of your self kick in and infuse your everyday awareness, the courage to change will follow.

CHAPTER 16

Nurturing the Positives

OF COURSE, CONFRONTING NEGATIVITIES has a highly positive spin-off. This is that energy, time and attention normally devoted to sustaining defensive behaviours is now freed up. In a very real sense, all that energy, time and attention is excess to the strict requirements of working to feed, clothe and house oneself and one's dependents. The now unused energy, time and attention is consequently available to be directed into fostering growth in the essence self's moving, emotional and intellectual centres and in realising the life plan. To help understand how this works, the layered self may be thought of as a system.

THE SELF AS A SYSTEM

In general, systems have (1) inputs, (2) stock which is the build-up of what arrives via the inputs, and (3) outputs which run down the stocks. A water reservoir is a simple system. Rivers, streams and rain water are the inputs that flow into the reservoir, its stock consists of the dammed water, and the output is the water that is allowed to flow out.

In the layered self, the inputs consist of what is perceived and experienced, the stocks are what the individual derives from those perceptions and experiences after processing them, and the outputs are words, behaviour, actions and projected feelings and thoughts.

However, where the layered self differs from other systems is that outputting stocks does not run them down. Instead, outputting stimulates further inputs from the environment. Furthermore, the quality of outputs affects the quality of the new inputs. This is seen in the way that focus on a particular activity or issue, let's say an engineering problem, results in further input around that problem. High level outputs in a professional environment generally stimulate high level new inputs. On the other hand, high level outputs in a low level environment will not result in the same high level inputs. However, and this is what makes the human being so fascinating, low level inputs may result in high quality being added to the experiential stock as a result of high quality processing of low level inputs. What makes this possible is the filtering that alters perceptual and experiential inputs in the very act of being received.

Human beings possess two fundamental filtering mechanisms: the hard-wired physiological filter provided by the configuration of the five senses and the nervous system and its brain, and the soft psychological filter provided by everyday awareness. Both human perceptual and experiential inputs and the resulting stock are profoundly impacted by these two filtering mechanisms.

For example, if a person's physiology is impaired he or she may not perceive colours or hear sounds, either partially or completely. So the received sensory inputs, along with all the moving, emotional and intellectual data associated with what is sensed, are less than the human norm. On the other hand, hunters train their senses so they can see or hear at a much higher level than is the human norm. In addition, their existing stock of experiences enables them to filter greater information out of sense data than a non-hunter would given the same data. So while there is a normal level of functionality, people's ability to receive and process sensory inputs varies significantly.

The psychological filtering that occurs within everyday awareness is even more complex. Every time human beings process sense data they draw on their stocks of existing experiences and knowledge, as in the case of the hunter. But they may also draw on biases, prejudices, fears, and prior bad experiences. Any or all of these then colour their perceptions. If a hunter was attacked by a wild animal last time he went hunting, that experience may lead him to be jumpy, imagining movement in shadows where there is none.

Accordingly, there is both positive and negative filtering. The latter occurs when negativities present in the experiential stock taint incoming sense data. Having one's house robbed and subsequently being suspicious of anyone near one's house is a simple example of this. Being molested sexually during childhood and that affecting one's adult sexual relations is a more complex example.

There is no need to list here all the ways that hard and soft filtering affect the build up of experiential stock. However, it is clear that the bane of everyday human existence, being defensive behaviours, seriously impacts first on what types and qualities of inputs the self allows in, and second on how those inputs are processed and filtered to build up experiential stocks.

In the case of Bill, on the occasion when his everyday awareness received a cue from his spiritual self, if he had been locked into his standby defensive mode he could easily have rejected the cue outright. Or, if he did accept it, he may have turned it around and interpreted the insight as his work colleagues attacking or seeking to belittle him. If he had done that, instead of the perception stirring him to change his behaviour it would have reinforced his behaviour and made him even more defensive. This indicates the subtlety and pervasiveness of the everyday self's psychological filtering. When one is immersed in it, one is asleep to the way it dictates one's behaviour.

That is another reason why those seeking to develop themselves need to purify their layered self. Without purification both their perceptions and their experiential stock are open to being tainted. Accordingly, building up positive experiential stocks depends on eliminating defensive and negative traits that taint everyday awareness, which itself colours and limits experiential inputs.

The other key aspect of systems relevant to mastering the art of incarnation is that many systems, especially biological systems, have a high level of self-organisation. They are able to adapt as inputs change, they learn new behaviours to cope with new kinds of inputs, and they generate new layers of complexity to process more complex inputs. As a result they are able to evolve as a system.

The five layered self is a goal-seeking self-organising system. Its goal is to learn and grow from experiences. Its self-organisation enables it to adapt. And its purpose is to contribute to the evolution of its ongoing spiritual self.

THE EVOLVING IDENTITY

Overall, spiritual evolution is a process in which spiritual identities undergo a series of incarnations in a human body in order to develop their potential. In the process they not only mature as identities, they also gain mastery over self-selected situations, processes and skill sets. Spiritual maturity results from the sowing, harvesting and processing of human experiences.

Two aspects have a significant impact on what occurs during this process. The first is that each spirit starts from a different place in terms of its initial conditions. Second, because each spiritual identity is a self-organising system, each has the capacity to adjust its inputs and the kinds of experiential stock it holds during the course of its multiple lives. Self-adjustment during the gathering of experiential stock contributes fundamentally to what a spiritual identity becomes. How so?

Each individual spirit starts from a different place, that is from different initial conditions, in the sense that it has a unique innate nature. We attempted earlier to give a taste of this unique nature when we described each spirit as consisting of the combination of core disposition, modality and secondary disposition. No two spirits are quite the same in the combination of these three elements. Indeed, some spirits diverge wildly from the statistical norm.

This means that when different spiritual identities receive exactly the same experiential inputs they filter them in very different ways. As a result they quite naturally build up very different kinds of experiential stock, even when they are living in the same situations as other individuals and undergoing very similar situations. We will provide an example.

If three individuals with the core dispositions of servant, artisan and warrior received the same experiential input, let's say news of protesters being batoned by police, the servant might go to help the injured, the artisan could write a song about it, and the warrior may choose to replace the injured on the front line or join the police force. Clearly, this is an overly simplistic example. But it indicates how the core disposition each draws from in order to process the same input may result in widely divergent responses. These responses in fact reflect differences not just in the core disposition, but in how that disposition filters the received news and the selected action.

Complexifying these responses even further is that each individual is striving to fulfil pre-selected life tasks. This means that life tasks and life goals may also impact on the way each individual responds to the news. So the servant may alternatively write a poem about the protests, the warrior could go help the injured, and the artisan might join the police – because those responses, while they diverge from simplistic interpretations of what motivates each core disposition, are consistent with their life plan this time round. Alternatively, all could ignore the news and carry on doing what they were already engaged in.

The point being made here is that each layered self, along with its attendant spirit, is a self-organising system. So each has the capacity to change its experiential inputs on the fly, so to speak, and to filter and select not only the types of experiences it has but also to choose the breadth, depth and intensity of each experience as it impacts on its everyday awareness. This means there is no set outcome from initial conditions. Whatever nature a spiritual identity has the very first time it is embodied in human form is no indication of what experiential stock it will accrue as a result of multiple incarnations. There is no set formula for what individuals will become based on what they start from.

To change the metaphor, each spirit may be thought of as being a seed that has the potential to blossom into a unique flower. The seed's characteristics are defined by its unique combination of core disposition, modality and secondary disposition. However, the particular environments the seed plants itself into life after life, the experiences it undergoes, and the ways it processes those experiences, all impact on the seed's nutrition and growth. Furthermore, the seed affects its own growth according to what it chooses to experience and what it decides to extract from those experiences. So what the flower will be like when it matures is far from a given. There is no way of predicting what the flower will be on the basis of the seed. The flower may be small and dowdy. Or it may be a gloriously coloured bloom. Which is not to make a judgement in favour of one over the other, for when examined more closely, the small and dowdy blossom may be intricate, exquisite and unique, while the gloriously coloured bloom may be one among millions.

Accordingly, some of the flower's eventual characteristics result from the seed's innate characteristics. But it is much more the case that the flower's final form reflects the individual's personal engagement with the opportunities offered by embodiment. Each individual's flowering reflects what they make of their largely self-selected life experiences. Nothing is dictated. Nothing is certain. So an individual's state of being when the cycle of incarnation comes to an end is very much in the hands of the individual concerned.

In relation to human incarnation, the proper answer to the question, What's in it for me? is: What do you want to put into it? The earlier you give energy, time and attention to reducing limiting negative traits and to nurturing the positive aspects of your self, the more you will become at the end.

CHAPTER 17

Addressing the Reality of Your Life

THE LINK BETWEEN THE SPIRIT and everyday awareness is closer than people realise. The truth is that the reality of your life reflects the reality of your ongoing spiritual identity, because each spirit is using incarnation to learn, grow and mature. This applies especially to circumstances, choices, people and tasks you feel compelled to embrace during your life. They are not present randomly. They have been selected by you, at the level of your spiritual self, to enable you to explore, process and understand whatever you are engaging with this time round.

A significant consequence is that by examining the circumstances of your life you can gain insight into your own spirit's intentions. Key life situations, dilemmas and choices offer clues as to what your life plan is, what tasks you have set yourself, and what goals you are here to achieve.

Of course, not everyone is conscious of this. But those whose awareness is locked into the activities of their body and socialised self, and as a consequence are not conscious of input from the spiritual level of their being, are no less spiritual beings than those who regularly pray, meditate, attend spiritual retreats, or honestly strive to harmonise their lives to whatever concept of God they revere. Indeed, atheists who are free of often restrictive religious concepts may be acting more in concert with their spiritual self's life plan than an overtly religious person. Naturally, the opposite may also be true. The fundamental difference between people does not lie in whether they are religious or not, or even whether they are overtly spiritual or not. The fundamental difference is in whether their everyday awareness is centred in their crystallised socialised self and its defensive strategies, or whether it is centred in their essence self and they are drawing on its life goal to largely live in accordance with their life plan. This applies whether they are aware of it or not.

Of course, complexifying this admittedly somewhat crude demarcation is that there are gradations in people's awareness of input from their spiritual self. Those who strive to establish and cultivate a conscious connection between their everyday awareness and their spiritual self, and who consciously seek to live in accordance with the goals set for this particular life journey, are clearly more deeply engaged with the task of becoming spiritual than those who follow inner cues while being somewhat hazy about where the cues come from, or who act on cues without being aware of their source. Then there is the situation of those who deny or ignore inner cues altogether, preferring to engage with their lives on just the physical and social levels.

While individuals certainly miss opportunities to learn and grow during their incarnations, this only occurs for a short time, whether within a life or across a brief series of lives. These individuals then shake themselves out of their torpor, intoxication, indulgence, or whatever is distracting them, and re-engage with the deeper impulses of their spiritual self in a manner consonant with their deep desire to experience what human incarnation offers. They refocus on achieving the goals they have set themselves.

This means that no one may be judged as being better or worse at making the most of the opportunities provided by incarnation. Everyone at some time misses opportunities, for whatever reason. And everyone eventually catches up with themselves and achieves what they choose to do. Nothing and no one is lost. It is just that some like to dawdle and smell the flowers. Or trample them. While others are in a hurry to fulfil goals and so completely ignore the flowers. Everyone has periods, lives even, when they dawdle, and others when they too are in a hurry.

BEING AND BECOMING

This book began by noting the difference between being a spirit and becoming spiritual. Being a spirit is a fact of human existence that is the case whether it is known and acknowledged or not. Becoming spiritual requires an intent to consciously engage with oneself on the essence level and to make a sustained effort to connect what occurs in one's everyday life with the intentions of one's spiritual self.

As was stated at the start, being a spirit is not difficult. It is a fact of your existence. However, becoming conscious of your spiritual self, becoming aware of your life plan and of the tasks you have set yourself to achieve, and consciously allowing your life to be driven by your life goal, is not so easily achieved. And yet it could be. It only requires the intention to do so, and then following the cues that will and do arrive from your deep self.

What makes this simple task so difficult for many is that there is a big issue with hearing inner cues. The problem is the presence of inner haze and static. Haze consists of the lack of inner focus that results from negativity and defensiveness. Inner static consists of the many often contradictory desires, emotions and thoughts that swirl around inside an individual's everyday awareness, pushing it in various directions. Inner haze and static cause an individual to hesitate and miss opportunities, or to not notice cues at all.

In order to hear inner cues individuals need to do much work to remove psychological factors that prevent cues from being heard. The purpose of this work is to sharpen the attention of the everyday awareness so that cues from the spiritual self may be heard, given they are subtle whispers in comparison to the comparatively coarse shouts of the body and socialised self. And given you cannot act on what you do not hear.

The purpose of incarnation is to live a life, with all that involves. Some may lose themselves in the intricacies of their experiences. Others may inwardly hold part of themselves back, sustaining the awareness that they are incarnated, that they possess a spiritual self, and even that they have had other lives, aspects of which they are drawing on in this life.

It needs to be made clear that, of the options of losing oneself in life or being self-aware, one is not better than the other. One approach is not spiritually good and the other spiritually bad, nor good or bad in any other sense. As we observed earlier, it is a fact that some people are mature and some are immature. That is, some individuals have incarnated a greater number of times than have others, have had more experiences, and as a result have had more opportunities to practise the art of being incarnated. Having used their experiences to develop rich experiential stocks, and then drawing much from them, each has matured as a spiritual identity. Incarnation is a case of practice makes perfect. Or, as we prefer to say, practice leads to mastery.

So those who are inexperienced and lack expertise in the art of incarnation, who lose themselves in their life experiences, and who therefore neither become, nor wish to become, spiritual, are never judged or looked down on. The simple fact is they are in the early stages of their cycles of incarnation. As they gain experience they will come to appreciate the opportunities provided by incarnation and gain mastery over the subtle connection between their spirit and their everyday awareness. They will inevitably mature in their own self-selected way. That is the nature of incarnation.

Accordingly, what is being offered here is a perspective on incarnation that is intended to be useful to those who are maturing as human spiritual identities, as the less mature are occupied with other issues. How may you discern whether or not you are sufficiently mature to benefit from this information? Simply by the fact that you have read to this point.

We need to add a caveat to that last statement. This caveat is that obtaining benefit on the essence and spiritual levels always depends on the purity of your intentions.

PURIFYING INTENTION

One of the fascinating psychological results of a spirit being embodied in the human five-layered self is that an intention can start from any part of the layered self and then be taken up and acted on by any other part. An individual may read information, or absorb a teaching, and respond to it on the essence and spiritual levels, to the degree that they decide either to turn their life around or journey deeper into what they have already discerned. On the other hand, the socialised self may pick up that same intention and divert it into the more superficial, self-limiting and even negative parts of the self.

For example, an individual may read the material offered here, find that it resonates with them on a deep level, begin to act on it, but then find their momentum is interrupted by fears of whether or not they are doing the right thing, or by thoughts that they are special for being open to these concepts. Or they may decide this information provides an opportunity to enhance status or to make money. In this way a spiritual response is diverted by the socialised self, and an intention to act that at first is initiated and driven by the momentum provided by the life goal is diverted into the momentum of the everyday self.

This is why working to purify your layered self is so important. Purification requires clarity of purpose and results in essence level development. Together, clarity, purification and development reduce the inner haze and static and help ensure that intentions emanating from deep levels are not diverted into, and ultimately nullified by, shallower levels within the layered self.

Gaining clarity about your intentions occurs as a result of observing your own inner reactions and desires and using those observations to discern from which part of the layered self those intentions emanate. Thus clarity is essential to making the most of any deeper intention. Of course, this also assumes that you act on what you observe, and that you use that momentum to eradicate fears and defensive behaviours from your psychological make-up.

LIFE IS A WAR

The task of becoming spiritual may be described as a war of momentums that plays out in the circumstances of your life. It is not an external war between you and your desires on the one hand and people around you who are preventing you from doing what you want on the other. Rather, the war is internal. The war is between the momentum of what your essence self, driven by its life goal, is striving to achieve, and the momentum of your crystallised everyday identity, driven as it is by fears and defensive behaviours that prevent the life goal from being achieved. For those who seek to bring their spiritual self's intentions to the fore, this war gives has serious ramifications.

You need to reach a turning point. This occurs when you decide to disengage from the momentum of the crystallised everyday identity and switch to the momentum of the essence self and its life goal. Reaching this turning point involves making an inner decision to change your inner perspective. Turning points may involve leaving your current situation, changing your job, or severing significant relationships. But more often it involves changing little or nothing externally. It hinges instead on changing how you go about living your life. This is indicated by the example of Bill. His turning point did not involve leaving his job, but rather working differently. In fact, leaving his place of work would have been a flight from confronting his own psychological limitations.

You need ongoing commitment. The inner war between momentums means everyone swings back and forth from one to the other. There are times of determination, when one deliberately works towards a goal. And there are times of stasis, when the goal becomes shrouded in fog, or disappears from view completely, and you are wrenched by doubts or fears. You may even consider your life to be a terrible mistake. Such swings are a natural consequence of shifting between the two momentums. However, the courage to continue is always available. You just need to learn to shift your attention from the negative and self-limiting feelings and thoughts, and instead remember the intention that is driving you towards your goal. Your attention will then jump back to the momentum of your essence self. With the attention no longer immersed in the syrupy sea of hopelessness, momentum will be regained and progress continue.

Be lighthearted. Everyone makes errors and mistakes. Everyone at times fails to achieve what they hoped to. Learning mastery at any task is complex because there are many facets that need to be recognised and explored. So whenever you fall, get up and try again. Don't allow the crystallised defensive self to sneak up and whip you over your failures. But neither go too far the other way and break your arm patting yourself on the back. Celebrate that you have an opportunity to try again, then move on with hope to the next task. That is the opportunity provided by incarnation. There is always another time to do it better. And to eventually get it right.

LIFE AS INTENTION

There is a saying that life is only as easy or as hard as you make it. It would be truer to say that life is only as easy or as hard as you *intend* it.

Some people's lives are complex and difficult. But this is not because they have been bad in previous lives, or because they are missing important character traits that would enable them to get on less jarringly with others. Rather, it is because they have decided to address complex issues, or because they have taken on a significant number of tasks which require considerable juggling expertise, expertise that sometimes fails them. As a result, they drop the ball and life becomes messy.

Other people do not have apparently easy lives because they have been what people think of as good and therefore deserve a sweeter ride. In fact, they may have had a difficult life last time round and so, in the interest of self-restoration, have effectively decided to sit this one out. Or they may need a caring undemanding environment in order to be exposed to those qualities so they may learn to integrate them into their layered self. Or they may have chosen to be incarnated into an elevated social position in which they are constantly told they are special in order to address self-limiting psychological traits such as self-preening, arrogance or attachment to status.

Looking at an individual's life from the outside gives no immediate insight into why that person has chosen that particular life and what precise issues they are using it to work through. Whether a life outwardly appears easy or difficult does not indicate whether internally that life journey is similarly easy or difficult. There is no automatic correlation between the two. Each person has specific issues, attitudes and tasks they are grappling with, at their own pace.

Sustained observation and acute analysis is required to appreciate the inner dimensions of anyone's life journey, whether your own or someone else's. Yet for your sustained focus and analysis to be effective, you require a conceptual framework designed to facilitate analysis. The concepts offered here have been devised for such an undertaking. The model of the five-layered self, the description of the spiritual self as containing a core disposition that is modified by modality and secondary disposition, the requirement to shift the focus of everyday awareness from the crystallised socialised self to the essence self, the identification of an essence level psychological life goal, and the idea that each individual has a life plan – all these are offered as interlinked concepts designed to cast light on the process of incarnation and the purpose of individual embodiment.

The war that each person is involved in, the conflict involved in shifting the attention of everyday awareness from the momentum of the crystallised socialised self to that of the spiritually shaped essence self, provides conditions for learning. Obstacles are selected, obstacles are grappled with, obstacles are overcome. In the process much is learned, maturity is developed, and mastery over the condition of being a spirit incarnated in a human body is achieved.

There is no set time frame for achieving mastery. There are no limits set on what may be accomplished – besides, of course, the physical and psychological limits implicit in human embodiment. There is nothing within the human realm that you cannot do. It all depends on your intent.

Every life is an achievement. Every life contributes to what, who and how you are as a spiritual identity. Everything you do counts towards the evolution of your ongoing spiritual identity.

Be assured also that no one gets away with anything, whether it involves what others do to you or what you do to others. Neither do you lose anything, ever. Whatever positive outcomes or values you achieve during any life echoes within your ongoing spiritual self. This life journey is what you have chosen, whether that choice was made pre-life or during the course of the life journey itself.

We wish you well in making the most of this life. May you fulfil your life plan and find your bliss!

Glossary

Agapé — Agapé is spiritual level love, the highest form of love. Agapé has no projected desire other than goodwill. When embodied individuals experience agapé emanating from high level spiritual sources it invariably invokes a state of serene peacefulness and contentment.

Aura — A field of multicoloured luminous and radiant energy around a person or object. The human aura functions as a channel of communication between those in the spiritual domain and the embodied spiritual identity.

Act of guidance — A spiritual level initiative to communicate with an embodied being. This initiative may be through the stimulation of an idea, by a fleeting or persistent internally visualised image, by apparent internal thought or speech formation, by a sensation, by psychokinesis (such as bringing one's attention to a useful book by pushing it off a shelf), and so on.

Agreements — For a karmic link to be resolved, the individuals involved need to be reincarnated in proximity to each other. So prior to incarnating individual spirits make an agreement to meet and work through whatever exists between them. Sometimes the agreement is for one to take on the role of antagonist and push the other, while at other times individuals agree to work alongside each other.

Attachment — Attachment is a by-product of identification. When a spiritual identity identifies with its body as being its self it also naturally becomes attached to the people, objects, places, situations and experiences that form the texture of its daily activities and interactions. These attachments are physical, social and psychological in nature.

Barrier of the everyday Everyday awareness is generated when the everyday identity is immersed in everyday life. It is limiting in the sense that it keeps human beings locked into a repetition of the familiar, the known, the comfortable, the safe. This repetition forms the barrier of the everyday.

Beliefs All beliefs remain unverified assumptions until they have been tested and it is determined whether or not they reflect reality. Validated beliefs become the basis of new knowledge. The growth from an inexperienced child level identity to a mature adult identity is reflected in the progress from believing to knowing.

Biological self Commonly known as the body, grounded in the human animal, the biological self's physical characteristics are shaped by genetic inheritance. It also contains and sustains the human sensory and nervous systems, along with the brain and its cognitive functions that process perceptions and so underpin everyday awareness.

Bliss Sense-based experience is pleasure, which is experienced at the level of the biological self. Longer term bliss is called happiness. It is experienced within the essence self. Bliss arises from the full expression of the spiritual self. Insofar as the spirit seeks to express itself to its satisfaction during the course of its life, it is seeking bliss.

Clarity The purpose of clarity is to identify limiting negative attitudes and behaviours so they may be purified. Perceiving yourself without being defensive, and without giving in to conditioned assumptions about yourself and how you are viewed by others, is a major undertaking. By adulthood the socialised self and the everyday identity it feeds are crystallised. Achieving clarity about this crystallised identity, and appreciating how it functions during the course of everyday living, is a difficult task. Clarity supports development.

Conditioned reactions Conditioned reactions are automatically performed responses to life situations. They consist of learned emotional responses, attitudes and ideas about the world, part of the defensive behaviours that develop during childhood and augmented during adult years. As they limit human functioning, they must be addressed and overcome

Core disposition There are seven core dispositions of spiritual identity. The Michael Teachings divide them into the metaphors of servant, artisan, warrior, scholar, sage, priest and king. The expression of each individual's core disposition is further modulated by modality and secondary disposition to create a unique identity. These three factors combined also predispose each individual to pursue a specific variety of bliss.

Courage Spiritual endeavours are not often thought of as requiring courage, but being courageous is a necessary preliminary to confronting one's limitations. Courage is a natural by-product of both the desire to change, cued by the spiritual self, and the momentum to realise the life plan that is driven by the essence self and its life goal. In this way, changing attitude, momentum and courage reinforce each other.

Crystallisation By the age of twenty-one, the nominative age of human maturity, the socialised self has crystallised into a rigid identity. What is crystallised are the psychological traits and behavioral coping strategies that it embraced in response to the impacts of family, community and culture while growing up. For most individuals, the crystallised socialised self provides their identity for the rest of their lives. Of course, the socialised self will dissolve when the body dies, so everyone breaks free of the socialised self at death. Breaking free before death is more problematic. The outright shattering of an individual's sense of personal identity would be so traumatic it would likely kill whoever tried to do so. Accordingly, rather than shattering the crystallised self, the psychospiritual approach is to chip away at the crystallisation, bit by bit, piece by piece. The practice of self-enquiry offers a process for doing so.

Defensive behaviours   When individuals are upset they strive to calm themselves by re-establishing their previous inner equilibrium. In unconsciously acting human beings this is achieved via the defensive behaviours of denying, justifying, deflecting and attacking. Initially formed during childhood, these four defensive behaviours manifest in all kinds of situations, at all levels of human interaction.

Development   When individuals are born their three essence self's centres do not automatically function to their full potential. They need to be developed. The developmental scale is broadly characterised as being from infant, to child, teen and adult. The centres develop as a result of consciously working with them. To reach their full potential they need to be purified of negative emotions, attitudes and behaviours. Development occurs most efficiently in tandem with the practice of clarity.

Devil   An illusion generated by projected human fear.

Deep essence   During the course of each incarnation a spiritual identity experiences human life via a sub-identity. When that sub-identity dies experiential data generated by the essence self during the course of its life is uploaded to the ongoing spiritual identity. Deep essence is the accumulation of all the essence level moving, emotional and intellectual qualities and traits that the spiritual identity has experienced, manifested and explored through its many sub-identities. Accordingly, deep essence refers to human level qualities, not spiritual level qualities.

Emotional centre   With the moving and intellectual centres, one of the three main components of the essence self. Emotions may be positive or negative. Positive emotions include love, compassion, gratitude and the ecstatic emotional states that mystics experience. Negative emotions include self-pity, anxiety, melancholy and despair. The moving part of the emotional centre enables you to appreciate the colours, textures and artistry of the world, and make your own contribution to them. The emotional part of the emotional centre is where emotions are experienced. This includes enabling you to enter into the feelings of others. The intellectual aspect of the emotional brain manifests as intuition, which facilitates the making of connections and usually occurs as spontaneous flashes of insight. No centre naturally functions to its highest potential. Negative emotions need to be addressed and overcome in order for the emotional centre to reach adult functioning.

Energetic self   This is an energetic complex that functions on several levels. It includes the energetic envelope that surrounds the body, known as the aura. It also includes energy centres, commonly called chakras, and energies associated with each of the moving, emotional and intellectual centres.

Essence self   The higher level functions of the human animal, characterised here as consisting of the three moving, emotional and intellectual centres. The essence self is where the growth of human abilities and identity occurs.

Everyday awareness   In ordinary terms, the level of awareness manifested by the alert human brain. In the terms designated here, everyday awareness is a function of the active parts of the biological, socialised and essence selves. One of the aims of embodiment is to imbue the everyday awareness with the intent and awareness of the spiritual self.

Everyday identity   The identity each individual maintains during daily life. Everyday identity changes only marginally as an individual grows from infant to child to teen to adult. Aspects of everyday identity are projected onto an individual by others, but most are constructed by individuals in response to growing up. Psychological impositions and trauma significantly influence the quality of everyday awareness. Everyday identity usually develops a momentum that remains the same through a life, unless it is worked on and adjusted.

Experimental spirituality   An approach to spirituality that treats beliefs and assumptions not as truths but as propositions that one needs to enquire into. This approach also involves perceiving your life as an experiment in consciousness, with you being the experimenter, using your own life to experience, learn and evolve as a spiritual identity.

Evolution   Personal spiritual evolution is a process in which identities undertake an extended series of incarnations to develop themselves. The goal is to deliberately sow, harvest and process human experiences in order to gain mastery of self-selected situations, processes and skill sets. The process of gaining mastery generates experiential data that helps the essence self grow during each incarnation. This essence level data is accumulated at the level of deep essence, contributing to the evolution of the spiritual self.

Fear   There are two fundamental sources of fear. The first is the existential fear a naive spiritual identity feels on first being embodied in the human domain and finds it is unable to control the body in which it dwells. The second level is the fear emanating from the old brain, an animal defense mechanism that manifests as flight or flight. This animal fear has been socialised over the eons and now manifests in subtle behaviours. As a result fear has become embedded in human culture, including fuelling religious beliefs. A variety of different socialised fears drive the psychological make-up of everyday identity. The Michael Teachings identity these seven fears as the fear of not having enough, of being vulnerable, of missing out, of being inadequate, of being worthless, of losing control, and of the new. Each socialised self is driven by one of these fears, which is usually selected prior to incarnation then reinforced during childhood experiences. One of these fundamental fears leads to the development of a corresponding chief feature. Self-calming and defensive behaviours are used to cover up fear, which then becomes deeply buried within the socialised self. As such, fear fuels all the factors that limit an individual's ability to make the most of opportunities. Fear limits growth. One's underlying fears needs to be addressed in order to facilitate inner growth.

Five-layered self   A model that proposes the human self consists of five layers, consisting of the biological self, the socialised self, the essence self, the energetic self and the spiritual self.

Forgetfulness   Forgetfulness is an advantage for spiritual identities when they incarnate because it enables them to forget what they experienced during previous incarnations, forget even that they *are* an embodied spiritual identity, so they can experience their current life in a fresh and open way. Forgetfulness is a disadvantage because it stops individuals from remembering why they are here, living the life they are, and interacting with those who play a key role in their life.

Growth   Human growth requires the right conditions. The body needs nutrition, while the socialised self needs language, education, nurturing. Developmental growth occurs at the level of the essence self. In order to grow, the essence self needs to express itself and requires repeated opportunities to practice its abilities. If any of these are deficient, individuals will not reach their growth potential in this life.

God   The universe was created. This creator may be called God, if one wishes to use that designation. This creator is not a person or personal. The human everyday awareness is incapable of comprehending the nature of the vast all that is, let alone the nature of the even vaster creator of all that is.

Identification   Identification is a state in which an individual's everyday awareness and sense of personal identity is limited to the physical experience of being a body. In reality, each human being consists of a spiritual consciousness using a body to experience life in the physical world, but identification leads human beings to think not only that they are a body, but that everyone else they interact with is also a body. The spiritual dimension of identity is forgotten. In this way identification reinforces forgetfulness.

Identity — Identity exists on many levels. External identity consists of bodily and socially constructed identity. Internal identity consists of the self-image one constructs for oneself. Essence level identity reflects practical, emotional and intellectual abilities and expertise. Everyday identity is the identity people project and protect during daily interactions. Underlying them all is spiritual identity, the ongoing identity that uses external, internal, essence and everyday identity to live a human existence.

Imagined deity — A projection onto reality by the human everyday awareness, a process which reduces the incomprehensible creator of all that is to human dimensions. A typical form of imagined deity is when the creator is reduced to the human bodily dimensions of Jesus, Krishna or of a "super person" of similar kind. As such, imagined deity is a projection of human wish fulfilment, in which human beings imagine an extra-natural father- or mother-like being who cares for them personally. They certainly are cared for, but it is by spiritual beings who, out of love, have taken on the task of nurturing the embodied. The creator is not directly involved.

Inner cues — Inner cues come from the spiritual self. They consist of impulses that manifest in the everyday awareness as feelings, thoughts or as an inexplicable urge to make a certain choice or to follow a particular line of activity. In general, inner cues help people fulfil their life plan.

Insights — Insights are obtained as a result of enquiring into what one observes. Psychologically, insights involve either appreciating how a particular emotion, attitude or behaviour came to be conditioned into one's make-up, or how they are expressed in a variety of different situations in daily life.

Intellectual centre — With the moving and emotional centres, one of the three main components of the essence self. The moving part of the intellectual brain, called the formatory apparatus, is an organiser. It organises, categorises and compares concepts. The emotional part of the intellectual centre manifests in the way human beings respond to the sight of stars in the night sky with awe, wonder at powerful and beautiful landscapes, and humility when contemplating the vastness of the stars in the night sky. The intellect of the intellectual centre manifests in humanity's most abstract forms of thinking. It identifies patterns, whether sub-atomic, biological, philosophic, artistic, theological, mechanical, electrical or cosmological in nature.

Intention Intention ultimately emanates from the spiritual self. All spiritual identities intend to use the experiences gained during their incarnation in a human body to learn, to transform their functioning at all levels of their layered self, to grow, and to evolve as a spiritual being. The life plan is the extension of a spiritual identity's intention into the essence self level within the human realm. Forgetfulness, identification, attachments, and negativities blunt intention.

Karma Karma consists of an action, that action's motivation, and its consequence: karma = motivation + action + consequence. These form a unit of karma. Karma results when one person impinges on another. There are three grades of impinging: minor, intermediate and major. Minor impinging requires a change of motivation and inner attitude. Major impinging requires the individuals concerned to meet in an incarnated state and resolve their issues. The resolution of intermediate impinging depends on circumstances. Dissolving negative motivations is crucial to resolving all levels of karma.

Knowledge Information obtained via direct perception and acquired during personal experience, that has been processed and verified. Verification may occur as a result of repeated obser-

	vations, and also via peer review, in which group members compare experiences and conclusions. Knowledge is key to vanquishing fear.
Life goal	The life goal is a psychological trait that functions at the essence level. It is a concept developed within the Michael Teachings, which identifies seven life goals: growth, revaluation, dominance, submission, acceptance, rejection and maintaining equilibrium.
Life lessons	Whenever individuals go through an experience, review it, and come to understand what they did correctly and what incorrectly, that experience becomes a life lesson. Life lessons come in many forms, may be short or long in duration, and occur in every kind of situation. They lead to mastery in any of the many fields of human endeavour. Reviewing experiences can happen while living a life, but most individuals extract life lessons after a life has been lived.
Life plan	A plan shaped by a spiritual identity prior to its incarnation in a body. The life plan provides the basis for the experiment that is anyone's life. Incarnated individuals have the choice of keeping to a life plan or of abandoning it during the course of a life. Part of the experiment that is incarnation is to see how the identity copes with what it has organised for itself to experience and learn during that life. Lives that abandon a life plan are not failed experiments. They are merely alternative experiments, and have equal value, because all experiences provide life lessons and so may feed an individual's evolution. Abandoned life plans are usually taken up again in subsequent incarnations.
Love	Love exists on multiple levels. There is the biological love of parents for offspring. There is the mutually dependent love mixed with sexual attraction depicted in stories of romance. And there is the altruistic love of an individual for others who are not part of his or her direct gene pool. The highest form of love is agapé.

GLOSSARY

Mastery — Mastery is gained in any aspect of human endeavour as a result of sustained application, in which one focuses attention on a limited range of experiences, develops skills appropriate to that context, learns from mistakes, and by degrees gains expertise. Mastery is gained as a spiritual identity incarnated in a human body when one's everyday awareness is suffused by the spiritual self and when one has learned to become deeply knowing and perfectly loving.

Maturity — The purpose of incarnation is for spiritual identities to use the opportunity to become mature. The process of maturing involves building skills and talents to a level of mastery and learning to navigate successfully through any and all human situations. Achieving these goals requires individuals to extract life lessons from experiences. The process of maturing is reflected in development at the essence self level. A mature human being is acknowledged as being loving, knowledgeable and wise. Maturity at the spiritual level results in individuals no longer needing to incarnate.

Meaning — Meaning is constructed within everyday awareness. Each species has an everyday awareness it uses to construct its own unique meanings from what it perceives. Flies construct fly meanings, dolphins construct dolphin meanings, eagles construct eagle meanings, and the human everyday awareness constructs human meanings. For human beings meanings involve processing perceived events, giving them significance, striving to understand what caused them, and ascribing to them purpose or purposelessness. However, when ascriptions of significance, understanding and purpose (or not) occur within the everyday awareness, and that awareness is functioning in its crystallised form, human meaning-making is inevitably skewed and limited.

Meditation — A state of inner or dual awareness which is achieved by practising one of many techniques that promote internal or external focus. The body may be kept still or in rhythmic movement for the duration of the state. Meditation is differentiated from sleep by continuous mental alertness. An essential function is it offers a way to establish a bridge between spiritual identity and everyday human identity.

Modality   Modality is layer that modulates the expression of a spiritual identity's core disposition. There are three modalities: inward, outward and expressive. A spirit dominated by the inward modality is naturally drawn to contemplative modes of responding to life experiences. A spirit dominated by the outward modality naturally tends towards giving themselves over to participating in life experiences, initiating actions. A spirit dominated by the expressive modality naturally seeks to give outward expression to inward thoughts and feelings. In practice, different percentages of each modality is present in each individual, contributing to their unique deep make-up.

Momentum   Each individual has two primary momentums in this life, one emanating from the everyday self and the second from the essence self. The everyday self's momentum results from the psychological mass generated by the five factors of culture, roles, routines, habitual behaviours and conditioned reactions. The positive result of this momentum is that it gives individuals the feeling that they are the same person from one day to the next. The negative result is that everyday momentum keeps an individual travelling along the same inner lanes for years on end, repeating the same thoughts, having the same feelings, and doing the same things. Alternative to the momentum of everyday identity is the momentum of the essence self and its life plan. Inner development requires individuals to jump momentums, from the everyday self to the essence self.

Motivation   Intention emanating from the spiritual self manifests within the essence self as motivation. Motivation must be sustained at the essence level in order to carry out any task, whether spiritually oriented or everyday. Spiritual intention remains constant, but motivation is impacted by an individual's reactions to life experiences, which are themselves impacted by the settings of the socialised and biological selves, and so waxes and wanes.

Moving centre   One of the three principal components of the essence self. The emotional part of the moving centre manifests in body-focused emotions, the two most common forms of which are instinctive and adrenal. Positive moving emotions include the physical joy derived from marching, dancing, playing sport or gardening. Instinctive emotions include those involved in mating and nurturing children. Adrenaline emotions are used in sport and physical confrontation. When the instinctive and adrenaline emotions reinforce each other – which they do in territorial and ownership disputes – they can become very powerful and potentially destructive. The intellect of the moving centre provides common sense, used to think through practical issues and problems.

Negativities   Consisting of negative emotions and attitudes, negativities are psychological obstacles that must be overcome in order for the layered self to function at its optimal level and to grow and evolve. Fear underpins all negativity.

Observation   Occurs when one part of the essence self observes another part of the self in operation in order to collect data. Typically, the intellect is used to observe one's own emotions in operation. Individuals often use their essence self's emotional centre to observe others' behaviour. This can offer useful, even correct, psychological insights. However, the problem with observing via the emotional centre is that judgement, or self-deprecation, or blame, or some other negative attitude is often embedded in the emotions and valid observations are caught up in subjective emotion. To be useful, observations need to be detached and non-judgemental.

This is why observing using the intellectual parts of either the intellectual or moving centre is preferred to using the emotional centre.

Obstacles In general, human beings do not learn as much when life goes easily and well. Rather, human beings learn best when they come up against obstacles and problems, and when they are confronted by their own limitations and mistakes. Each individual perceives obstacles and responds to them in different ways. This difference is mostly due to variations in psychological make-up. The life plan is organised so key obstacles arrive at specific stages in their life so life lessons may be learned. Sometimes these obstacles are so well integrated into daily living that they appear as just another problem to be dealt with. At other times the obstacle arrives from left field and creates a huge disturbance, sending the individual in a new, unanticipated direction.

Psychological mass The everyday identity is constituted of biological drives, essence processes and activities, and socially conditioned attitudes, outlook and behavioural coping mechanisms. These combine to create a psychological mass that causes individuals to move at a particular momentum through life, fending off others by denying, justifying, deflecting or attacking while self-calming in preferred ways in order to maintain its momentum. Inner development requires that this psychological mass be broken down. Self-enquiry provides the means for achieving this.

Purification Clarity, purification and development occur hand-in-hand. Clarity helps identify the negativities that are impacting on essence level functioning, while purification eliminates those negativities so further development may take place. Purification requires intense inner work characterised as self-enquiry. With clarity and development, purification facilitates essence level growth and spiritual evolution.

GLOSSARY

Original sin   An imaginary concept that is part of the socialised control/inhibition mechanism by the Christian religion control believers and sustains their status in relation to the divine. Believers use the doctrine of original sin to inhibit themselves in the choices they make during the course of their life. Many individuals cling to the concept of original sin because it deflects attention away from their own limitations and inadequacies, ascribing their deficiencies to a purely imagined situation.

Reincarnation   Reincarnation is axiomatic to this experimental view of human existence. Spiritual identities choose to experience embodied human life in order to learn and grow. The cycle of incarnation is repeated until the spiritual identity learns what it came to learn, and has grown in the ways it choose. The cycle then comes to a close and the next phase of non-embodied evolution is embarked on.

Scientific method   An experimentally-oriented process used to obtain new knowledge about what happens in the world. When applied to spiritual practices it facilitates the acquisition of new knowledge that has been extracted from, and verified within, the context of personal experience.

Scientistic outlook   A set of assumptions that underpin scientific enquiry. Includes the assumption that only matter exists, that there is no realm apart from or beyond the material world, that human consciousness is entirely a by-product of the biological and chemical processes of the body's central nervous system and its brain, that no non-material spiritual or supernatural entities exist, and that what cannot be explained in rational and naturalistic terms does not exist. As an approach to physical reality it is certainly useful, but it becomes a liability when it is adopted as a dogma and advocated with a fervour bordering on the religious.

Secondary disposition   Each individual spirit possesses a three-fold nature of core disposition, modality and secondary disposition.

The secondary disposition consists of one of servant, artisan, warrior, scholar, sage, priest or king. Secondary disposition influences the way core disposition manifests. In the human realm secondary disposition manifests more directly when interacting with others, while primary core disposition remains hidden. The result is that if an individual has a core disposition of warrior and a secondary disposition of sage, others are much more likely to observe the sage performative characteristics and much less likely to see the deeper warrior drives.

Self-calming   Self-calming generally follows a shock of some kind in which fear or similar intense emotions are stirred up. It is a psychological mechanism that helps an upset identity return to its accustomed inward state. Self-calming behaviour varies, depending on psychological make-up, but may include eating, drinking, smoking, exercise, playing, shopping, becoming angry, becoming violent, or walking away. All cover over and repress the intense inner response that triggered the need to self-calm in the first place. Self-calming must be overcome to pursue self-enquiry.

Self-defensiveness   Behaviours the everyday identity uses to cope with emotionally upsetting, confronting or invasive life situations. Defensive behaviours are driven by fears of various kinds and manifest in denying, justifying, deflecting and attacking. The particular patterns of defensive behaviours present in an individual's psychological make-up are primarily shaped during the childhood and teen years. They become crystallised by the onset of adulthood, if not earlier, and dictate how individuals defend their everyday identity in social situations, often for the rest of their life.

Self-enquiry   The process of observing one's inner make-up, analysing psychological processes, identifying positive, negative and self-limiting attitudes, behaviours and characteristics, and working on them to foster personal development.

Socialised Self	The socialised self consists of a psychological and behavioural layer within the five-layered self that is shaped by the social conditions into which an individual is born. Language, family, education, social norms, work, opportunities, and so on all contribute to the formation of the socialised self. Where the biological self is shaped genetically, the socialised self is shaped by social and environmental conditions and by the way the individual responds psychologically to those conditions. As such, the socialised self is a social construct. Self-image is largely a function of the socialised self, resulting in the socialised self underpinning everyday identity for most people.
Spiritual self	The spiritual self is the individual's core spiritual consciousness within the layered self. The spiritual self is in turn a fragment of a larger spiritual identity. The spiritual self's intent, wherever it is and whatever it experiences, is to learn and grow. Spiritual identity isn't static. It evolves as it learns from its experiences. The spiritual self's goal is wisdom, becoming a more loving and knowing identity.
Sub-identity	In each life a spiritual identity enters a body and takes on the genetically inherited and psychologically conditioned characteristics that together form a unique human sub-identity. This sub-identity exists for the duration of that lifetime, providing a spiritual identity with the opportunity to explore pre-selected situations and experiences. At the end of its cycle of incarnations, a spiritual identity's human maturity exists as the life lessons it has accumulated via all its sub-identities.
Transformation	The spiritual self's intention when it incarnates in the human domain is always to transform its five-layered self. Life lessons feed inner transformation. As the layered self is transformed, it grows. This growth in turn feeds the evolution of the ongoing spiritual identity.
Truth	There are various kinds of truths. Assumed truths include

inherited and conditioned beliefs and assumptions. When beliefs and assumptions are tested they lead to new knowledge that may be viewed as providing newly discovered truths. However, these are provisional truths. Provisional truths are truths that will do for now, but that will eventually be supplanted by new discoveries and even newer provisional truths. Those who consider they know The Truth are using what they think they know to hide behind. What they are driven by is an underlying fear.

Turning points　Effectively, a turning point disrupts a life's momentum and turns it in a new direction. Usually such a disruption is key to the realisation of the life plan and involves shifting a life's primary momentum from the everyday self to the essence self. For most people, turning points changing involve a confrontation. External confrontation occurs when one becomes profoundly unhappy with life circumstances, occupation, relationships, marriage, etc. Internal confrontation involves individuals becoming profoundly unhappy with the way they function psychologically or with how they are living their life. Whether the confrontation is external or internal, individuals reach a key moment of decision, in which they are confronted with their own inadequacies and pains. Often the impulse to confront whatever is inadequate emanates from the spiritual self and is experienced as a series of inner cues.

Understanding　Understanding is achieved as a result of processing the knowledge extracted from life lessons. Because life lessons involve confronting one's own limitations and fears, knowledge and understanding are always hard won. The understanding individuals extract from their experiences during the course of their life occurs at the level of the essence self. Understanding is also extracted from experiences by the spiritual self, after a life is over and during the post-life review process.

War of momentums   The task of becoming spiritual may be described as involving a war of momentums that plays out in the circumstances of your life. It is not an external war between you and your desires on the one hand and people around you who are preventing you from getting what you want on the other. Rather, the war is internal. The war is between the momentum of what the essence self is striving to achieve by putting its life plan into action, and the momentum of the crystallised socialised identity, driven as it is by fears and defensive behaviours that prevent the life goal from being achieved. Each life necessarily involves periods in one momentum dominates, then the other. However, as an identity matures it is better able to sustain its awareness within the momentum of the essence self and so is less disorientated by the opposing momentum of the socialised self. This maturing process occurs both within each individual life and across the arc of all lives.

www.ingramcontent.com/pod-product-compliance
Lightning Source LLC
Chambersburg PA
CBHW021126300426

44113CB00006B/305